THE POCKET IDIOT'S GUIDE™ TO

Being the Father of the Bride

By Jennifer Lata Rung

ALPHA

A member of Penguin Group (USA) Inc.

THE POCKET IDIOT'S GUIDE TO and Design are registered trademarks of Penguin Group (USA) Inc.

International Standard Book Number: 1-59257-059-3
Library of Congress Catalog Card Number: 2003100696

05   04   03   8   7   6   5   4   3   2   1

Interpretation of the printing code: The rightmost number of the first series of numbers is the year of the book's printing; the rightmost number of the second series of numbers is the number of the book's printing. For example, a printing code of 03-1 shows that the first printing occurred in 2003.

Printed in the United States of America

Note: This publication contains the opinions and ideas of its author. It is intended to provide helpful and informative material on the subject matter covered. It is sold with the understanding that the author and publisher are not engaged in rendering professional services in the book. If the reader requires personal assistance or advice, a competent professional should be consulted.

The author and publisher specifically disclaim any responsibility for any liability, loss, or risk, personal or otherwise, which is incurred as a consequence, directly or indirectly, of the use and application of any of the contents of this book.

Most Alpha books are available at special quantity discounts for bulk purchases for sales promotions, premiums, fund-raising, or educational use. Special books, or book excerpts, can also be created to fit specific needs.

For details, write: Special Markets, Alpha Books, 375 Hudson Street, New York, NY 10014.

Contents

Introduction

The father of the bride—historically, the most neglected of all the wedding day participants. Until, that is, all those wedding-related credit card bills begin clogging your mailbox. But we know you're more than just a big open wallet. You're a human being, with feelings, concerns, and preferences of your own. So why, then, does tradition dictate that for your daughter's wedding, you're expected to pay a lot, but plan very little? To "host" an event you've had little say about? Never has carte blanche come with so few strings attached.

This book is meant to change all that and to help you take charge. A bit of a stretch, you say? Then at the very least you'll learn the difference between a boutonniere and a bridal bouquet, and how to best handle being a host. In fact, you may wish to consider this book your travel guide into the foreign, often dangerous territory of the wedding industry. Though you enter this heart of darkness with trepidation, you'll have plenty to boast about once you've emerged from it.

Times are changing. Brides and grooms are planning—and paying for—more and more of their wedding expenses. At the same time, many families still follow formal tradition dictating that the bride's family pays the lion's share of wedding expenses. In this confusing and ever-changing climate, where do you stand? What must you contribute, financially? Even more important, how do you deal with this young, new alpha male in your household? And what are some best practices for traditional dad duties like escorting your daughter down the aisle, the wedding toast, and the father-daughter dance? This book will answer all these questions … and many more.

So read ahead. And get ready to conquer a whole new land.

Extras

The sidebars in this book are designed to offer bite-sized pieces of information that every father of the bride should know. Decoding them is easy. Simply refer to the following for guidance:

> ### "Pop"ositions
>
> "Pop"ositions offer tips to help you, dad, do just about anything wedding-related even better. Whether you need help dancing like Fred Astaire or to deal with the groom's family, "Pop"ositions provide quick strategies to have you stepping out—or sidestepping— in no time.

> ### Dad's Definitions
>
> Why is everyone at the dinner table suddenly speaking Swahili? Oh wait, that's just wedding jargon. Dad's Definitions aim to simplify and explain these foreign ideas in terms every man can understand.

Paternal Precautions

You're a dad with a grown daughter. No doubt "precaution" has become your middle name. But when it comes to wedding hazards, you've stepped into foreign territory. Paternal Precautions will let you know all the perils that may befall you.

Father Figures

Is this a party or a money pit? Father Figures will provide you with strategic ways to save money—as well as advice about things to avoid, whether you're paying with cash, check, credit card, or your first-born grandchild.

Acknowledgments

Thanks to Jessica Faust, Mike Sanders, and Suzanne LeVert for all their hard work on the book.

Trademarks

All terms mentioned in this book that are known to be or are suspected of being trademarks or service marks have been appropriately capitalized. Alpha Books and Penguin Group (USA) Inc. cannot attest to the accuracy of this information. Use of a term in this book should not be regarded as affecting the validity of any trademark or service mark.

Chapter 1

She's Leaving the Nest

In This Chapter

- Why her wedding is so important to her
- What is your role?
- How to stay close to your daughter
- Welcoming your new son-in-law

So your little girl is getting married. Whether this news triggers a spring in your step or a turn to your stomach is pretty much irrelevant. What is relevant, however, is how you handle it. And handle it, you must. Because (almost) no matter what, this wedding is going to happen and it's up to you to decide whether you'd like the next 6 months (or 12, or 18) to be somewhat tolerable … or absolute torture.

Where to start? Unlike that of the bride, her mother, her sister, her best friend, or even the groom, your role is murky. In fact, you probably have very little idea of what you should be doing while the bride and her mother feverishly choose the date, the venue, their dresses, the caterer, as well as the 700 additional details they will need to organize. As for the groom, he's got everything he can handle simply deciding where he'd like to celebrate his bachelor party, and whether he should choose Bali or Bermuda to take your daughter on the honeymoon. And the groom's parents' role? Well, everyone knows their task is simply to sit back and zip a lip. But what about you, dad? How will you endure this season in purgatory?

Historically, the bride's dad had little involvement in planning the wedding, which often led to aimlessness, confusion, and maybe even isolation for dads everywhere. However, as is true for the groom, fathers have become more involved in wedding planning, and that's a good thing. Although you'll probably feel like you're playing the role of Gilligan to your wife and daughter's Skipper, you can still contribute valuable opinions and be part of planning one of the most important—and expensive—events you've probably ever been involved in.

Her Most Perfect Day

If you're like most other members of your generation, you probably played little part in your own wedding day besides showing up to the ceremony on time, smiling and kissing a few hundred cheeks, and dancing the night away with your new bride. Most likely you were not really involved in planning the whole affair, which was left to your fiancée and more likely, her mother. Moreover, let's face it, that was a long time ago, and you probably don't remember the planning stress, in-law conflict, maybe even your own wedding song. Heck, even remembering your anniversary date strains your memory bank every year.

"Pop"ositions

Remember your daughter's prom? Well multiply that preparation by 20, and you'll understand what you're in store for. Luckily, this time she knows who her date will be …

In case the manic post-engagement energy in your household hasn't already dictated this same sentiment loud and clear, I'm here to remind you that you can't take your daughter's wedding lightly. But why is this one day so important to her, you ask? What could possibly prompt all this stress and effort? The following may offer some clues into the psyche of your household's newest little princess-to-be:

- She's in love.
- She's in love with love (possibly even a stronger driving force than simply being in love).
- She's been fantasizing about this day since a long time ago. Like her single digit birthdays.

- She believes this is the most important day of her life.
- She enviously observed her older sister get married … and capture all the attention.
- She needs to outdo her best friend's wedding.
- She secretly (or overtly) wants to be queen for a day.
- The seemingly long wait toward wife-hood is finally over.

For all these reasons, your daughter's wedding is a ritualistic rite of passage. Like a tribal male's celebration after his first kill, this event has got to be big. Bold. And memorable. Because (with any luck) it's strictly a one-time event, which means it's gotta be good.

So what does this mean for you? First, it means you must try to take this whole thing seriously. There may be times you'll question your daughter's behavior—her daylong crying jag when the DJ cancels, for instance, or the hysterical arguments with her mother over the centerpieces. You'll experience the strong desire to put this all into perspective for her: Is a 10-course meal really necessary when people in the world are starving? Is a disagreement over the bridesmaids' dresses really worth a life-long grudge against her sister? Despite the fact that you will, in reality, be the only voice of reason in your family unit, you must suspend your own reality for a while and dwell in the temporary insanity of your family's female world. It's called self-preservation, and this book will provide you with a leg up on the other poor dads out there sadly left to fend for themselves.

Just What Type of Dad Are You?

Self-preservation aside, it's necessary to figure out sooner than later your desired degree of involvement in this whole affair. You may wish to begin scheduling more business trips than normal over the next few months. Or you may truly want to be more involved in the wedding planning process (particularly if you're this shindig's rainmaker). To discover your true, innermost intentions, take the following quiz.

1. When your daughter announced her engagement, you:
    a. Felt genuine happiness that she found a decent guy.
    b. Felt relief that she'd finally be leaving the nest.
    c. Hoped her fiancé has a strong constitution.
    d. Contacted your cop buddy to do a background check on the groom … and his friends.

2. When you and your wife plan a party, you:
    a. Run details about menu, guest list, activities, etc., through your mind for weeks.

    b. Think little about it but help out the day of the party.

    c. Leave the details to her and show up when you're told.

    d. Contemplate leaving town.

3. When you think about your own wedding, you remember:

    a. Almost every detail, as you helped plan it.

    b. The date.

    c. The honeymoon. Oh yeah.

    d. As little as possible.

4. How do you feel about marriage?

    a. Can't imagine life without it.

    b. A good institution, although hard work.

    c. A necessary evil.

    d. It should be outlawed.

5. How would you describe your financial style?

    a. I am frugal at times, and will splurge at others.

    b. I don't deal with finances; my wife handles them.

    c. I believe that anyone will rip you off if you give them the opportunity.

    d. I am keenly aware of where every cent I make goes.

Scoring:

Mostly A's: You are well balanced, detail-oriented and would be a good candidate for getting more involved than the typical dad in your daughter's wedding. You are most likely quite rational when it comes to money and emotion, a perfect combination for planning a wedding. Have fun and lend your logic!

Mostly B's: You're the typical laissez faire dad; you don't get overly involved with the girls' affairs. However, your daughter's wedding could be the perfect time to show some interest and, by doing so, grow closer to her.

Mostly C's: You are a bit cynical and world-weary. This wedding stuff may not be your thing at all. However, you may wish to feign interest and get involved in some aspects of the wedding, particularly in the financial realm. Try not to be too heavy-handed if you wish to avoid major pre-wedding conflict.

Mostly D's: You're pretty much hopeless. Don't like marriage, don't like your future son-in-law, and don't like spending money. Your best bet? Observe from a distance and try not to rain too hard on your daughter's parade.

So You Want to Be Involved

You've taken the quiz and you've earned a C or above. You've decided that you want to be involved in this extravaganza, or at the very least understand what's going on around you. After all, even aging boy scouts know the value of being prepared.

Paternal Precautions

If you plan to get involved in the wedding planning, expect one of two reactions from your daughter: excitement that you want to be a big part of her special day, or complete dread that you will pressure her to do things your way.

Or maybe you scored a "D" but would still like to know the absolute minimum in store for you. The following two lists outline potential duties for each type of dad, so you can put on your thinking cap or at the very least, begin planning your escape.

Minimalist Dad

These are the bare bones duties for the traditional dad:

- Pays for some or all of the wedding costs.
- Cordially meets his daughter's fiancé's parents prior to the wedding.
- Discusses wedding finances with his daughter's fiancé's parents, if necessary.
- Escorts his daughter down the aisle, if requested.
- Acts as host at the wedding, including participating in the receiving line.

- Takes part in the father-daughter dance.
- Dances with bride's mother or his escort.
- Gives a wedding-day toast.
- Helps with post-wedding business, such as paying vendors, signing paperwork, etc.

"Pop"ositions

If you're a divorced dad or a stepdad, you may find yourself being asked to share the traditional duties. Look to your daughter for guidance and try to support her decisions.

Uber-Dad

This list includes those extra areas the more socially aggressive dad may find himself—or choose to become—involved in.

- Helping set a budget.
- Throwing an engagement party.
- Attending the bachelor party.
- Helping create a guest list.
- Helping create the seating plan.
- Helping choose or secure a ceremony site.
- Helping choose or secure a reception site.
- Helping choose or secure musical entertainment.
- Choosing or making suggestions for his formal clothing.

- Helping find adequate wedding-day transportation (time to call in the chips from his Ferrari-owning friend).
- Helping find a photographer and videographer.
- Picking up and transporting out-of-town guests as they arrive at the airport, or arranging for their transportation.
- Making maps to and from relevant locations, including to the ceremony and reception sites (may be included in invitation).
- Choosing the reception menu (he may be part of a pre-wedding "tasting" event hosted by the caterer).
- Choosing a wedding gift for the happy couple.
- Assisting with honeymoon costs
- Assisting with finding them a place to live (that old real estate connection may come in handy here).

Losing a Daughter

Of course, we haven't even touched on the emotional issues involved in "giving away" your daughter. No matter how old she is, you can't quite get that vision of a sweet, pig-tailed, innocent 5-year old out of your mind, the girl you raised, protected, and loved since she was at her most vulnerable. Giving your blessing to her marriage may feel somewhat akin to sending her to the wolves. After all, you're not only a dad, you're also a man. How do you handle any feelings of loss or sadness, or even apprehension about the decision she's made? The following sections may provide a few hints.

Support, not Criticism

It's entirely possible you're not altogether sure of her fiancé, and that's okay. What's not okay, however, is repeatedly haranguing her about it (unless, of course, he displays threatening or destructive behavior, in which case all bets are off). Unfortunately, it's difficult, if not impossible, to convince an adult child of anything unless they want to be convinced, especially if they're in the throws of romantic love.

If you have serious doubts about their compatibility, try to be diplomatic—and logical—in your reasoning. State your case once, and let her take or dismiss your advice. Unfortunately, if you're too heavy-handed, you may turn her away completely, which will do neither of you any good in the long run.

A Helping Hand

There are lots of ways to help your daughter during the engagement period, and they're not just limited to wedding planning. Support her by providing an escape when things get too stressful. Do something you've always enjoyed together like fishing, golfing, going to a museum, or just taking a walk. Provide a listening (nonjudgmental) ear when she needs to vent frustrations. Maybe even give her some insight into a man's perspective on marriage, or offer advice on what you believe makes a marriage strong. This is not only an exciting time for her, but also an emotional and scary one as she makes one of her most important life decisions. As someone who's been though it, you are an invaluable, and probably under-utilized, resource to her. The bottom-line? This pre-wedding time can help you two grow closer rather than further apart.

New Traditions

If your daughter is leaving the nest—literally—you may worry you'll seldom see her once she's out of the house. Even if she's been living on her own for a while, you may be apprehensive about the changes in store once she's married. That's why now's the time to think about establishing some mini-family traditions to ensure you spend time together in the future. For example, make plans to run together in the morning a couple times a week, or share Sunday dinner as a family. Knowing that there are established times during which you'll still see your daughter can help ease separation anxiety—for you and the entire family.

Gaining a Son (in-Law)

If you're lucky, you've come to believe the sentiment that marriage is not about losing a daughter, but rather gaining a son. Unfortunately, many fathers are not this fortunate when their daughters decide to marry. In the last section we covered your strategies for dealing with your daughter if you question her choice of mates, but now we've got to address your relationship with your future son-in-law. After all, he's not just marrying your daughter, he's marrying your family, too. Used wisely, some one-on-one contact can provide a strong foundation for your future expectations of him. As your daughter's father, you don't need to be shy in expressing yourself.

Embrace the "Request for Her Hand"

Possibly, your future son-in-law has already confronted you to receive your blessing in marriage, the old request for "her hand" in marriage. This is an old-fashioned tradition not practiced nearly enough anymore, in many dads' opinions. If you're lucky enough to be welcoming a young man with manners, however, you should expect some effort on his part to speak to you and your daughter's mother, out of respect for your entire family. He may do this before or after the official engagement, and really, it's never too late for him to have a chat with you. This can be a great opportunity to have a real man-to-man talk with him. He will, no doubt, nervously approach you expecting the worst. But this conversation can be adult, open, and mature rather than intimidating. You may appropriately ask him what his goals are for the future, his views on marriage, whether he plans to raise a family—these are all legitimate topics, particularly if *he* has approached *you*. It will give you a good idea of where his head is, and it may give him the impetus to begin thinking more seriously about these issues. If he knows you care, it will keep him on his toes.

"Pop"ositions

If your daughter and her fiancé live out of town, make an effort to visit them a few times—or invite them to visit at your home—before the wedding. It will give you a better opportunity to get to know the newest member of your family.

Get to Know Him

If this man is your daughter's childhood sweetheart, he's probably already an unofficial member of your clan. But if he's relatively new to the family, the engagement period is the ideal time to really get to know him better, both within the family context and one-on-one. To get to know him better, ask him to golf with two of your friends or family members, or make it a twosome. Go hunting together. Do whatever sporting activity you both enjoy. Take the opportunity to drag him along on an errand or two. Invite him to your club outing. The point is, get to know him as a person, not just as your daughter's boyfriend or fiancé. You may discover you have a real connection or at least the foundation for a life-long mutual respect.

Hold Him Accountable

All the warm and fuzzy bonding aside, there's also no better time than now to start setting some ground rules—or at least healthy family patterns—for the future. If he sits at your house watching football all day while you sweat it out doing yard work, put him to work occasionally. Let him know that you expect him to enthusiastically take part in family events. In other words, don't let him get away with behavior now that you don't want to see him repeat in the future.

A girl has no better ally than her father. No matter how independent or strong she may be, she's always counted on you to protect her, steer her in the right direction, and provide a port in a storm. And even though she may now be ceding some of those responsibilities to her fiancé, it's comforting for her to know you'll always be there for her, no matter what. Use this time leading up to the wedding to seal those expectations and you'll grow closer to your daughter than ever before.

The Least You Need to Know

- Accepting how important her wedding day is to your daughter will help you stay sane and productive during the planning stages.
- There are plenty of tasks to do that even a dad who wants to take a back seat can handle.

- Planning a wedding and participating in pre-wedding events offer plenty of opportunities to bond with your future son-in-law.

Chapter 2

It's Wedding Season

In This Chapter

- Understanding pre-wedding events
- A who's who of wedding day vendors
- Honored wedding-day positions defined

There's a chance you may have an intimate knowledge of everything wedding-related. But unless you're employed as a florist, a pastry chef, or a caterer, it's more likely wedding planning is about as foreign to you as who's on Oprah every afternoon or other typical chick stuff.

This chapter will provide an overview of what to expect over the next few months. It should help you develop a working knowledge of what to expect during the weeks and months leading up to the wedding, including a who's who of all the new people in your life. You will receive a "least you need to know" on each topic and a bunch of relevant definitions so you'll be able to keep up with conversations and (sort of) understand what your daughter, wife, and family members are actually talking about from time to time.

The Engagement Period

If you think the wedding simply takes place on one day, think again. A wedding takes place over an entire extended season (or more) of fun. It's kinda like football. All year you look forward to the Super Bowl (wedding day), but of course there's a strong lead-in with the pre-season (courting), regular season (engagement party, wedding planning), and playoffs (showers, bachelor and bachelorette parties, and rehearsal dinner). With this kind of anticipation, no wonder there's so much excitement surrounding the wedding day. Plus, a wedding costs almost as much as one of those 30-second Super Bowl ads.

So what can you expect, step by step? You probably have a vague notion of the definition and reasoning behind some of these practices, but in case you're a true novice, here goes!

The Engagement Party

The engagement party is simply an opportunity to celebrate the upcoming nuptials of your daughter and her fiancé. This party can be a great way to bring both families together for the first time, or to formally introduce your future son-in-law to your network of friends and family. Alternatively, the groom's parents may also throw an engagement party for the same reasons, and many couples are throwing their own engagement parties to bring friends and family together. This means there may be multiple parties for the happy couple.

Of course, the engagement party is strictly optional. If you do decide to throw an engagement party, you should probably plan it soon after the engagement announcement, so as not to coincide with later social functions like bridal showers, and bachelor and bachelorette parties.

What should the engagement party entail? It can take any tone you wish, ranging from a casual back-yard gathering to a formal catered event. Many guests will bring gifts to the engagement party though, if the bride and groom prefer, "no gifts" can be specified on the invitation.

The Bridal Showers

Traditionally, the bridal shower has been strictly the province of women and has consisted of a gathering of those closest to the bride to share a meal and "shower" her with household essentials. Usually, the maid of honor and bridesmaids throw these showers, though in many areas of the country it's becoming common for the bride's mother to host them as well. The bride may have multiple showers, as her different contingents of friends and family honor her. These showers may include one thrown by the groom's family, the bride's close girl-friends (also known as a "*personal shower*"), or a shower hosted by the bride's co-workers.

Dad's Definitions

Steer clear of attending a **personal shower,** lest you care to witness your daughter receiving "intimate" wedding gifts like lingerie. This is typically a small and close-knit affair hosted by the bride's sisters or girlfriends.

Showers generally last a few hours and may be held at someone's home, a restaurant, or a catering hall. They usually take place on a weekend afternoon, during which women share a luncheon or brunch followed by a gift-opening session and other activities. The bride typically receives gifts that serve as a foundation for a new household, stuff like china, flatware, towels, sheets, small appliances, and cookware. Usually she will have registered for these gifts at a department or specialty store. Registering means the bride and groom choose the items they specifically want or need for their household, in the right sizes, styles, and colors. This can be done at a store or stores of their choosing. You will inevitably hear your daughter discussing the ins-and-outs of registering, which can be an incredibly daunting and time-consuming task. Where to register? What to choose? Is there too much or too little? Trust me, choosing the gifts that others will buy you can be a very stressful task, dad.

"Pop"ositions

A nice, fatherly thing to do to help out with your daughter's bridal shower is to show up at the tail end to help pack gifts into the car ... and say hello to all the ladies. To make a real splash, send your daughter flowers or a flower corsage prior to the start of the shower. (Though you may have some competition here from the groom.)

More relevant to you than the "girl shower," however, is the growing popularity of a "Jack and Jill" or co-ed shower, to which both men and women are invited. These are typically evening parties at which much of the usual shower activity takes place—cocktails and food, followed by the rapt opening of gifts, in this case, by the bride and groom. Even though there are probably things you'd rather be doing, remember that this event is for your daughter. At least you're not the groom, sweating under the hot lights trying to figure out just who Great Aunt Mildred actually is!

The Bachelor Party

Unless you've been living on Venus, this affair hardly needs explanation. If the groom is having a large, raucous affair, you will inevitably be invited to the party. If you're reasonably close, you may also be invited to a more intimate gathering, like a dinner out. Most likely, it will be a gathering of the groom, his friends and male family members, plus you and your close male family members. Enjoy yourself and get to know new people. With any luck, there will be no activity that will prompt you to begin cleaning your gun collection any time soon.

The Bachelorette Party

The bachelorette party is a relatively recent phenomenon that most likely developed as a response to all the fun the boys were having at their guys-only galas. Usually planned by the bridesmaids at the behest of the bride, bachelorette parties have been known to range from a quiet dinner to a spa weekend to a wild and crazy night on the town. Unless you are called upon to bail an errant bridesmaid out of jail, you will have minimal involvement in this event. This is probably best, unless you enjoy watching your daughter drunkenly sipping from phallic-shaped straws. (Yes, there is a whole industry of bachelorette-party accessories, too.)

The Rehearsal Dinner

This gathering is the dinner that follows the wedding rehearsal and is typically held one or two evenings before the wedding day. Traditionally, it is the responsibility of the groom's parents to plan and host the rehearsal dinner, but with lines blurring in recent years, it's possible that this duty, too, may fall to your family. If so, understand that this party, like the engagement party, can be as casual or formal as you wish. Included on the guest list are the bride and groom, their immediate families and escorts/spouses, the wedding party and their escorts/spouses, and optionally, any out of town guests who have made the trip in order to attend the wedding.

The rehearsal dinner is typically an intimate, more relaxed warm-up to the next day's events, and often includes speeches or toasts by the groom and/or bride, and the groom's father, if he is hosting the event. If you are hosting the event, feel free to say a few words yourself—but save the best for the wedding day toast. A fun tradition is to open the floor to any guests who'd like to make their own toasts; these "impromptu" speeches are often some of most memorable events of the wedding.

The Wedding Day Players

Just who are all these people vying for your family's hard-earned dollars? Who, exactly, is behind this increased frequency of phone call activity, at all hours of the day and night?

To put it bluntly, they are members of your daughter's new, albeit temporary, cult. Like a traditional cult, it is the wedding cult's duty to brainwash the bride into believing their respective canons—that she cannot think of living without this wedding cake, or this flower, or this dress. In other words, it is the job of these people to justify and reaffirm her temporary wedding insanity, no matter what the cost, emotional or financial. Beware, but don't lose too much sleep. They will release her (and, in turn, you) from their spell as soon as that last bill has been paid.

Of course, you may have some control over the choice of vendors, if you so choose. You may decide to help your daughter "shop" for services to get the best quality or the best deals, or you may simply wish to use your veto power with out-of-control vendors—*if* you hold the purse strings.

The Wedding Coordinator

If your daughter has hired a wedding coordinator to help plan and organize the details of her wedding, this person will inevitably become an extended part of your family during the engagement period. Though the degree of involvement varies, the wedding coordinator will help her scout ceremony and reception sites and make recommendations for all the wedding vendors. He/she will also be responsible on the day of the wedding for ensuring everyone shows up on time, has delivered what they've promised, and behaves as they are supposed to.

 "Pop"ositions

Rent "The Wedding Planner," the hit movie starring Jennifer Lopez, for a fuller view of the wedding coordinator's duties. (No pun intended)

A wedding coordinator is an expense that can pay for itself—both financially and mentally. Due to the sheer volume of parties they've planned, wedding coordinators often can secure vendor discounts and will know the ins and outs of the industry, which offer a real advantage, especially in a larger city where vendor options are endless. A wedding coordinator also provides a nonemotional, objective point of view that can provide a buffer between your daughter and her mother; she/he can also provide a much-needed resource if your daughter is planning the wedding by herself.

The Caterer

The caterer is in charge of food and drink for the reception. The caterer may be affiliated with the hall or restaurant itself, or may be a mobile operation that can set up and cater at any venue. Caterers generally offer certain specialties that may depend on the type of food you want, the size of the event (very large or very intimate), and the degree of formality (casual, semi-formal, or formal).

The Musicians

You may find yourself employing a relatively large number of musicians for each of the wedding-day stages, including the ceremony (e.g., organists, string quartet, vocalist), the cocktail hour (harpist, pianist), the dinner hour (strolling violinist, flautist), and dancing (band or DJ). Who plays at what event is obviously up to the wedding decision-makers, as well as the wedding budget. You can find musicians through recommendations by friends, the yellow pages, your church or synagogue, even your local university's music department.

The Photographer and Videographer

On the actual wedding day, you'll have more contact with the photographer and videographer than with any other vendor. Because they will be in your faces all day doing their jobs, encourage your daughter to choose professionals with a good camera-side manner (i.e., people who won't annoy you too much), as well as the requisite artistry and skill. Be sure to see his or her prior work before signing on. Photographers can be strong in some areas and weak in others: Some are great at formal, posed portraits, for instance, while others are better at photojournalism (candid, unposed shots). Your best bet is to help your daughter envision how she wants her final wedding album to look, then choose the professional accordingly.

The Florist

The florist is the person responsible for the bridal bouquet, the bridesmaids' bouquets, the *boutonnieres* (men's lapel flowers), the decorative ceremony arrangements, and the reception centerpieces and decorative flowers. Again, be sure to choose someone reputable to ensure the proper product will arrive, and arrive on time.

Dad's Definitions

The **boutonniere** is a single bloom or bud attached to the left lapel of a man's jacket. These flowers are typically worn by you, the groom, the attendants, ushers, and the bride's father.

The Baker

The baker will bake the cake according to your daughter's specifications. Typically, wedding cakes are multitiered sensations with elaborate icing and detailing. They are usually prepared with either a traditional buttercream frosting or fondant style, which is icing that appears as if it is carved from stone (and some critics argue, also tastes that way) with a very smooth surface and elaborate detail. The baker may also make a groom's cake, a popular addition in some areas of the country. A groom's cake usually is a rich chocolate treat meant to complement a lighter wedding cake. The key to choosing the right baker is to find someone reputable who will deliver the wedding cake on time and in one piece.

Father Figures

Eggs, flour, and butter have never been so swanky. When it comes to the wedding cake, brace yourself for the bottom line.

The Driver

When shopping for wedding transportation, don't forget to ask who the driver will be. Be sure to confirm you'll be driven by a certified, licensed driver so you'll all arrive at your destination(s) safe and sound. Ask the proprietor for documentation.

Whether your daughter hires a limo, a trolley, or a small bus to transport the wedding party from place to place, it's important to tip the driver at the end of the trip. Taking care of the driver is a responsibility ideal for you, dad, to take on, as the bride and groom may be distracted from doing so amid all the festivities. You can arrange this with the groom in advance.

The Officiant

If the bride and groom will be having a religious ceremony, no doubt they may already have someone in mind to perform the ceremony—a church pastor, a rabbi, or other minister. If not, they may ask you or the groom's parents for recommendations if one of you has a close relationship with a clergy member.

Otherwise, the bride and groom should seek recommendations from other friends and family, particularly if it's going to be a secular ceremony and they have no one in particular in mind to officiate. Be sure the chosen officiant is legally authorized to perform the ceremony; for example, contrary to popular belief, ship captains are *not* automatically authorized to perform weddings.

No matter who will be officiating the ceremony, it's polite to invite the officiant to both the rehearsal dinner and wedding. Religious officiants may be asked to say a blessing or toast before the meal.

Wedding Day Honorees

There are also plenty of other, nonpaid wedding day players who are included as honored guests of the wedding. You'll recognize them by their cloned satin or taffeta dresses, or their ill-fitting rented monkey suits. You may wish to make a special point to greet these honored guests, many or most of whom you probably will already know. You may offer advice about who your daughter and soon-to-be son-in-law choose to fill these roles, but for the most part, you just have to know who goes where, when, and why.

The Maid of Honor

The maid of honor (if she's unmarried) or matron of honor (if she's married) is the bride's right-hand gal. (Some brides choose to have both a maid of honor and a matron of honor.) This right-hand person serves as the bride's moral support during the entire engagement period, and will help ensure things run smoothly the day of the wedding. Typically, the bride chooses her sister, another close family member, or a close friend to hold the honored position.

Specifically, the maid of honor is in charge of planning and helping to finance the bridal shower;

helping the bride shop for bridesmaid's dresses; helping to keep the bridesmaids organized and informed; attending all pre-wedding parties; and assisting the bride with her dress and other personal functions on the day of the wedding. Of course, many maids of honor do much more than this, helping the bride each step of the way with wedding planning, registering, pre-party planning and, of course, emotional support.

Bridesmaids

As the maid of honor has assumed more responsibility during the wedding period, over the years, a bridesmaid's role has become more and more symbolic. However, there are some tasks she is responsible for during the engagement period and wedding, including helping plan and (possibly) finance the bridal shower; helping plan (and possibly finance) the bachelorette party; attending all pre-wedding parties; purchasing the bridesmaids' dress designated by the bride; and participating in wedding day traditions including preceding the bride as she walks down the aisle. Of course, the bride may request other help from her bridesmaids, including help in wedding planning and helping to run wedding errands. Bridesmaids may also act as party ambassadors, leading the way for guests to the dance floor and providing general party revelry.

Typically the bride chooses a number of her close female family members and girlfriends to serve as bridesmaids. She may also include her groom's sisters or close family members if she so wishes. The

average number of bridesmaids is 4 to 5, but the
bride may choose to have many more (I've seen
12), or many less (one honor attendant is sometimes all that's desired).

The Best Man

Like the maid of honor is to the bride, the best
man is typically someone very close to the groom,
such as his closest male relative or friend. The best
man has an important—and public—role in the
wedding, and as such should be appointed with
care. In addition to helping the groom with any
pre-wedding planning or errands (things like shopping for formal clothes or scouting out bands), the
best man is also charged with planning the bachelor party. In addition, the best man is in charge of
holding (and protecting) the wedding rings prior to
the ceremony, helping with general wedding-day
troubleshooting, and most important, will deliver
the first wedding-day toast (preceding or following
the reception meal).

Groomsmen/Ushers

Groomsmen or ushers (the terms are often used
interchangeably) are made up of the groom's closest male friends and relatives. The number of
groomsmen typically matches the number of
bridesmaids, though this is certainly not manda-
tory. Groomsmen provide general moral support to
the groom during the engagement period, attend
pre-wedding parties, and, in some cases, help to
plan the bachelor party.

On the wedding day, the groomsmen are in charge of seating guests at the ceremony site based upon their family affiliation—bride's family and friends to the left, groom's to the right (as you are facing the proceedings from behind the seats or pews). Specific groomsmen should be hand-picked to walk honored guests down the aisle, including the mothers and grandmothers of the bride and groom.

If the bride will use an aisle runner, the groomsmen are also in charge of unrolling it immediately prior to the bridal party's walk down the aisle. Again, the bride and groom should choose these groomsmen to perform these tasks during the wedding rehearsal. Groomsmen are also charged with escorting the bridesmaids on their retreat down the aisle following the ceremony. They may also be asked to dance the first dance with their bridesmaid "partner." (What a chore.)

Flower Girl and Ring Bearer

The flower girl and ring bearer are those adorable little dressed up children you've seen at weddings who hesitantly walk down the aisle immediately before the bride. The flower girl strews flower petals in the bride's path, while the ring bearer's duties are largely self-explanatory he carries the wedding rings on a small satin pillow (though this can be symbolic, if the bride and groom don't want a 4-year-old in charge of thousands of dollars of jewelry).

Other Honor Attendants

The bride and groom may also honor other close friends or relatives with wedding-day duties such as performing ceremony readings or providing unique talents like singing or playing a musical instrument during the ceremony or reception.

So now you know the who's who and the what's what of weddings, or at least have a general working knowledge of what to expect in the weeks and months leading up the wedding. In the next few chapters we'll get more involved in your role as father of the bride, covering topics such as finances, interfamily communication strategies, and how to master your own wedding-day duties.

The Least You Need to Know

- Learning the cast of characters will keep you in the loop during the planning phase and the wedding itself.

- Choose your professionals with care. Doing so will save you much time and trouble down the road.

- Understanding everyone's wedding-day duties will allow you to pitch in and offer guidance when things get hectic.

- You may wish to supervise your daughter's wedding-day decisions, to be sure she doesn't go overboard with out-of-control expenses.

Chapter 3

Step-by-Step Planning: An Organized Strategy

In This Chapter

- Setting the wedding date
- Determining the guest list
- Ceremony and reception planning

Even if you don't expect to be very involved in actually planning the wedding, it'll help if you have a little knowledge about what exactly needs to be accomplished before and during the big day. Why do you need to know? Think of it this way: Say you and your buddies are huge football fans and you've got tickets to the Super Bowl. Your wife is coming along, too, but she doesn't know the first thing about football—and she doesn't much care, either. Chances are she'll be bored and ignored because the group will think she's a party pooper when really she's just uninformed and thus overwhelmed and uninterested.

Well, the wedding is the Super Bowl of social events in your daughter's life—and if you're an under-informed dad, you'll be ignored—and it's never fun to be ignored. After this chapter's crash course in the business of wedding planning, you may find yourself enjoying the trip a little bit more, or at the very least, understanding what everyone's talking about at the dinner table. Best case scenario? You may even find you enjoy some aspects of this new foreign sport.

Getting Down to Business

Before the actual wedding planning can begin, there are a couple key decisions your daughter—and your family—must make. These decisions will control all planning and details that come thereafter, including the choice of venue, vendors, and most important, vittles.

Day In, Day Out

As simple as it sounds, setting the wedding date can be complicated by many factors. While emotion and excitement may be leading your daughter and her fiancé to believe the sooner the wedding takes place, the better, there are some practicalities to consider as well. You can help the happy couple settle on a date by considering the following:

- Budget. No matter who pays, it may take a little time to put together the funds necessary to throw the desired shindig. A longer

engagement—a year to 18 months, for
instance—can provide a nice buffer to help
the financier (which may be you, dad) to
avoid going into major credit card debt.
Indeed, a longer engagement provides the
opportunity to comfortably set aside funds
on a monthly basis, avoiding the astronomi-
cal interest fees you'd incur by funding the
entire party with a credit card. In addition,
certain seasons—or specific dates—can
prove less expensive than other higher-
demand times. See Chapter 5 for more on
choosing bargain dates.

"Pop"ositions

As the bride and groom set the date, let
them know if you have any conflicts, such
as business trips or other obligations, right
away. It will help them avoid having to
change the date in the future.

- Season. Most brides have an idea of the season in which they'd like to marry: Spring
  and summer weddings offer the possibility
  of great outdoor spaces, fall is perfect for
  gorgeous color and scenery, and winter
  offers the charm of a cozy setting. The season will obviously be a major consideration
  when choosing a date.

- Career conflicts. Career conflicts may put
  some limitations on what date is chosen. In

other words, if the groom is a tax accountant, the wedding couple will probably want to avoid dates in March or April. If he's a house painter, summer's out of the question. Teacher? The school calendar may put certain dates out of bounds. Even though your daughter's seasonal fantasy is very important, gently urge her to consider career or education conflicts very seriously as they can add unnecessary—and unwelcome—stress to wedding and honeymoon planning.

- Social conflicts. Your daughter also may find herself limited by other obligations or upcoming events, such as the weddings of friends and family members or the pregnancy of a close friend or family member (e.g., it's a good idea to avoid choosing her matron of honor's due date for her wedding day!). She should also be sensitive to the obligations of those closest to her. If you and your wife go away with friends every Labor Day weekend, for instance, she may wish to take that into account. Or if her grandparents from the South have trouble handling cold weather, avoiding the winter months might be wise. Your daughter's objective should be to consider other's obligations and/or limitations, in addition to her own.

- Distance. If one or both halves of the happy couple live in a town other than the one in

which the wedding will take place, they may
wish to add some extra time to the engagement to accommodate travel arrangements.
A trip or two prior to the wedding will
probably be necessary to arrange party
details, fittings, attend bridal showers, etc.

Dollars and Sense

Once the date is set, the next step in the wedding
planning process is to determine a budget.
Obviously, the first and most crucial decision concerns where the money will come from. Your family, the groom's family, or the wedding couple may
be funding this party, or it may be a combination of
some or all of you. For more information about
budgeting details, including who pays for what,
average costs, and financing tips, see Chapters 4
and 5.

Once you establish your budget, including settling
on a bottom line figure, as well as agreeing upon
estimated line items—you'll find it easier to carry
out all your remaining tasks, including spending all
that money!

See You in Church!

Another important, but somewhat simpler, task to
tackle is planning the wedding ceremony. Because
ceremonies differ so greatly from couple to couple,
the following ceremony checklist aims to cover all
contingencies and items to consider.

- Deciding upon a religious or secular ceremony. Obviously, this is an extremely personal and potentially difficult decision. If your daughter does not share your family's faith, or if she is marrying someone of a different faith, it may be especially complicated. Discuss the possibilities with your daughter, but ultimately leave the decision to her and her fiancé. Try to support the outcome, whether or not it corresponds with your own belief system.

 Paternal Precautions _____

> One of the most incendiary issues your family may face surrounds the wedding ceremony, which involves the broader issues of religion, ethnicity, heritage, and tradition. Communication about these matters is vital. See Chapter 9 for a more in-depth exploration of the topic.

- Choosing a ceremony site. Choices include a place of worship such as a church, temple, or mosque, a hall or banquet facility, or an "alternative" or creative site like a hot air balloon, a ski slope, or a golf course.

- Acquiring a marriage license. In some states, a marriage license is only good for a finite number of days after it is issued. The task of obtaining one in a timely matter falls to the groom to perform, who should research all limitations or legal parameters. A friendly reminder from you, dad—or even a little help on the research end—would probably be welcome.

- Choosing a ceremony officiant. The wedding officiant can be a priest, rabbi, minister, justice of the peace, or any individual with legal authority from the state.

- Purchasing the wedding rings. Presumably the groom has already given your daughter an engagement ring, so it's now time for them to shop for his-and-hers wedding rings. If there is a family heirloom earmarked for your daughter, now is the time to inform her or present the gift; the rings may need to be resized or reset to complement her engagement ring.

- Choosing ceremony music. If you're holding the ceremony in a place of worship, there may be a pre-determined list of songs to choose from, as with most Catholic weddings. If not, the couple may wish to hire vocalists or musicians such as an organist, string quartet, or trumpeter, or play pre-recorded music.

- Choosing readings, poems, etc. Again, if you've decided upon a religious ceremony, there may be a choice among pre-determined readings. If not, the couple can craft their own unique and personal ceremony by hand-picking readings, passages from books, song quotes—anything goes.

- Writing vows. Many wedding couples take advantage of this attractive option. Instead of going with the standard, traditional vows, they write their own to further personalize their unique ceremony.

- Incorporating ethnic or religious traditions. Many ethnic groups have their own special wedding customs. A Greek Orthodox wedding, for instance, embodies the seven traditional elements (including the blessing of the rings, the joining of hands, and the crowning, among others). If it's an African American wedding, the couple may include a tradition called "jumping the broom," which involves the bride and groom literally jumping over a specially decorated broom to seal their bond of marriage. Be a wise and knowing ambassador to your own ethnic heritage and teach your daughter about traditions from your own family or ethnicity. She may wish to include them.

The Reception

Because the wedding ceremony itself consists largely of a simple exchange of vows and the ensuing assumption of a legal commitment between two people, the bulk of wedding day planning actually involves the reception, not the ceremony.

Here's where you can play a big role, dad, because there will be a deluge of details to deal with. You can start out by helping with tasks that most interest you or those that you can lend some special expertise. Perhaps you can arrange wedding day transportation, for instance, or scout out musicians or DJ's for the reception. Keep in mind that some tasks will demand your input, such as helping to determine the guest list or shopping for formal clothing.

Regardless of whether you're intimately involved or not in the following decisions, it's information you should know. This knowledge might allow you to empathize with (i.e., not disown) your daughter when she exhibits symptoms of hysteria as these details start getting out of control.

Scouting Out Reception Sites

You may be interested in helping the wedding couple find the right site for the reception and may even want to suggest a few yourself. Presumably you've been around the block enough to have visited some of the nicer places in town, and can report on details such as food and bar quality, service, and possibly price. Your daughter will welcome tapping into your experience for suggestions and opinions as she begins the search for prospective locations.

Possible sites include banquet halls, restaurants, hotel ballrooms, country clubs, historical buildings, museums or galleries, or a winery. Other options include outdoor venues such as national or state parks or beaches, passenger yachts, your home (sorry dad!), a friend or family member's home—anywhere where quantities of people can gather, eat, drink, and celebrate in relative comfort. More and more couples are throwing weddings at unusual or alternative sites, so don't be too surprised if your daughter wishes to throw a *theme wedding* that demands an unusual location.

> ### Dad's Definitions
>
> A **theme wedding** is any wedding that incorporates an overriding concept or creative idea. Examples of theme weddings include medieval weddings, 1920's weddings, underwater weddings, Victorian weddings, or holiday weddings such as Valentine's, Halloween or Christmas soirees.

If you're helping to scout reception sites, remember that the service is just as important as the aesthetics. A wedding at a seaside resort may provide the perfect atmosphere, but if the food or service is lackluster the whole party will suffer. Be sure to get recommendations and/or references before forking over a down payment.

Of course, your site may not include an affiliated caterer, so you'll need to research this independent vendor the same way you'd research a location with its own caterer. In other words, be sure to choose a reliable, experienced service provider with strong references.

Depending upon the reception site you choose, you may also need to consider equipment rental, such as tables, chairs, dishware, cutlery, serving dishes, bar ware, and linens. Obviously banquet halls and restaurants whose business is catering will already have these items, but if the wedding is being held at an outdoor or other nontraditional site, these items will need to rented separately.

Father Figures

Though it may seem less expensive to throw a wedding at a site other than a hall or restaurant (your home, for instance), equipment rental fees, catering, bar and server fees can really add up. Be sure to do the math before committing to this course of action.

Kickin' It Up a Notch

Deciding upon the food and bar can be among the most difficult decisions to make in wedding planning, if only because every guest will definitely notice both. If you're helping to choose the food, you will need to consider the following:

- Time of day. Obviously, a steak dinner at noon isn't the most appropriate dish—but a steak salad might be. Indeed, the time of day will be the biggest factor in your menu decision. Keep in mind that you're not necessarily bound to the traditional evening reception; depending on the time of day, you may decide upon a breakfast, lunch, brunch, dinner or cocktails/hors d'oeuvres reception.

- Budget. Sure, you'd love to fund a nine-course feast, but your budget only allows for three. And though the truffle-topped tenderloin sounds amazing, you'll have to settle for chicken picatta. Even if you can't afford the most decadent dishes, you can still impress your guests. In the end, more important than what you serve is how it's prepared. A great piece of chicken will always be more appreciated than a tough piece of steak. Shop around for a caterer who can prepare any meal well.

- Wedding style. Will your daughter be having a buffet, food stations, or a sit-down meal? Buffet and food stations involve guests serving themselves; sit-down meals are a bit more formal. Buffets are typically comprised of a number of entrees, side dishes, salads, bread and condiments. Food stations are usually more creative in presentation. Typically each station will have its own themed dish, such as a fajita station, a stir fry station, a baked potato station, or a meat carving station, which are set up in various areas of the room rather than in one central location. Sit-down meals usually consist of a number of courses, such as salad, soup, entrée, and dessert. The more creative the caterer, the more unique any of these serving styles can be.

Father Figures _____

Another popular myth is that a buffet is always less expensive than a sit-down meal. This is simply untrue. It all depends on the items chosen, as well as the amount of food served.

● Ethnic choices. The incorporation of ethnic tradition into the wedding may also dictate menu choice. A traditional Italian wedding, for instance, may serve regional specialties; an African American wedding may include traditional Southern–American or African fare. If there is a combination of ethnic traditions, menu choices from both cultures may be featured, such as an entrée inspired from the bride's heritage and dessert from the groom's.

No matter what the fare, your caterer or restaurant should host a tasting event, at which your daughter, her fiancé, and one or two family members can taste test a number of menu choices in advance. This is fun (and usually included in the price of the wedding) so lobby your daughter to include you!

Guest List

One of the most stressful parts of planning a wedding is forming the guest list. You will inevitably have a part in this aspect of planning, as there are bound to be certain friends, relatives, and associates you wish to include. One of the most common problems—and reasons creating the guest list can be so stressful—is that there are usually many more guests that you'd *like* to invite than you *can* invite, typically due to budgetary concerns. And while you may feel entitled to invite all the guests you'd like if you're footing the bill, the bride and groom will also feel strongly about having their chosen guests present—it is their wedding day, after all.

There are certain strategies your family can adopt when forming the guest list. The first is to decide on an arbitrary number, then whittle down the list from there. If you need to eliminate a significant number of guests, the first to go should generally be work associates (unless they are also personal friends). Relatives should be the last to go, although you can decide to keep it somewhat contained by keeping it within your immediate family, omitting more distant or removed family members. (One rule to consider may be if the bride and groom have never met them, they're taken off the list.) In addition, you may wish to limit the number of your own friends, though you'll surely be tempted to issue payback for all *their* kids' weddings you've been forced to attend over the years.

The key to settling on a final guest list is compromise. If you simply cannot omit inviting certain people but are limited by budget, play with the figures. Save money elsewhere by serving a more limited menu, or a lower shelf bar. If you feel the bride and groom have an unmanageable list of friends they'd like to invite (and you're paying) tell them they can pay for additional guests above and beyond a certain number (and watch how quickly that list whittles down).

"Pop"ositions

If invitations are sent out early enough, and you begin getting "no" replies, you may consider sending out additional invitations to those who didn't quite make the first cut. (But try to keep this under wraps ...)

Don't forget that you'll also need to consider the groom's family's guest list. Assuming you and yours are paying for the wedding, start out by giving them a number to work with (most polite is to give them half the total number). If they have a particularly large family or network of friends that surpasses this allotted number, you can discuss it from there—perhaps they'll offer to contribute to the cause. On the contrary, if the groom's family is splitting the bill with you from the beginning, it's presumed you'll make these decisions together. See Chapter 9 for in-depth coverage on in-law diplomacy.

Choosing Vendors

In Chapter 2 we addressed just who the wedding day vendors are, including the photographer, videographer, musicians, florist, bakery, and transportation provider, with some quick strategies on choosing all of them. If you're concerned about cutting costs (and who isn't?) we cover money-saving strategies in Chapter 5. More than likely, your daughter will already have a short list of some possible vendors, based on recommendations from friends and family, advertising, or other word-of-mouth. If you have any recommendations based on your experience—the name of a bakery that makes amazing cheesecake, for instance, or the car company that leases antique Rolls-Royces—feel free to put them on the table.

As tempting as it may be to get overly involved in any aspect of the planning, try not to pressure your daughter too much ... she'd like to feel as if she has some control over her own wedding. Keep in mind she's probably experiencing a great deal of pressure from the groom, her mother, her future mother-in-law, and her friends already. However, if you're paying, you do have ultimate veto power. Obviously, this takes a fine balance of caring father/smart consumer ... and some of these expenses you simply won't understand (Two thousand dollars for a dress she'll wear once? Thousands more for flowers with a one-day life span?) For a deeper understanding of just what these things cost and their relative value, continue to Chapter 4.

The Least You Need to Know

- Setting a wedding date means taking into consideration the schedules of everyone involved.

- Two important and fun jobs dads can tackle are scouting out a reception site and making recommendations for music.

- The key to creating the guest list is having a willingness to compromise by all parties involved.

- There are countless options when planning a wedding that go beyond the traditional sit-down style evening reception.

Chapter 4

Show Me the Money

In This Chapter

- Who pays for what?
- Wedding costs: national averages
- Types of weddings
- Setting the budget

As we've discussed, there are a lot of uncertainties and contingencies when it comes to wedding finances, characterized by a lot of if/then scenarios. For example, "if you're paying," "if the groom's family is sharing expenses," and "if the bride and groom are contributing" are common uncertainties. But which of these "what ifs" is proper? Who should ultimately pay and contribute to the wedding expenses, and for what items? How do the rules of etiquette apply to a changing world, one in which daughters aren't necessarily young and penniless and grooms may be more financially established than their own fathers?

This chapter aims to cover traditional expectations along with today's realities to find a method of financing that makes everyone comfortable.

Who Pays for What?

The most widely believed and accepted wedding tradition holds that the bride's family pays the lion's share of the wedding costs. Why? It turns out that this tradition evolved from the age-old practice of offering dowries. Instead of giving goats and cows to the groom's family in exchange for taking on their daughter as a financial burden, nowadays the bride's family simply pays for the wedding, which, by today's standards, is an equally burdensome expense.

Of course, most twenty-first century brides are less of a burden than they are an asset to today's households, pulling in their own share of the bacon and often living on their own for some years before they marry. In the past 20 years, the average age of first marriages for females rose from 22 to 25.1 (up from 20.3 following World War II). The bride who leaves the protection of her family home straight to being cared for and supported by her husband has largely ceased to exist. More likely, she will have graduated college or entered the job force, and will be somewhat self-sufficient by the time she marries. So why the discrepancy between tradition and reality?

That's just the nature of tradition. It took hundreds of years to become a commonly practiced behavior, so it'll probably also take more than a few years for the "accepted" manner of behavior and etiquette to change as well.

There is hope, however. Sociological changes over the last 20 to 30 years regarding family and gender have already produced a subtle psychological effect on wedding planning. Though many brides' families still cover wedding costs, more and more couples are paying for some—or all—of the weddings themselves. Once they are out of their parents' home and making money themselves, many brides and grooms feel there is no reason for their parents to be responsible for their wedding or other expenses. If this is the case in your family, lucky you. You've raised a daughter who is independent, self-sufficient, and sensitive to the needs of others.

No matter what your daughter's situation, however, you may still feel strongly about paying for and hosting the wedding; like helping pay for college, you may feel it's just what parents are supposed to do. And certainly it's a wonderful gift if you're able to give it, especially as your daughter and her new husband are making the effort to establish a strong foundation together.

Regardless of your motivations, it helps to have a traditional template of "what is expected." The following chart can provide some initial parameters regarding who's expected to pay for which wedding expenses, according to formally accepted etiquette.

Who Pays for What

Expense	Responsibility
Invitations/Wedding stationery	Bride and/or family
Bride's attire	Bride and/or family
Bride's rings	Groom and/or family
Groom's ring	Bride and/or family
Engagement party	Both families may host parties
Officiant fees	Groom and/or family
Groom's attire	Groom and/or family
Limousine	Bride and/or family
Bachelor party	Groom, his family, and/or best man and ushers
Rehearsal dinner	Groom and/or family
Reception	Bride and/or family
Wedding cake	Bride and/or family
Music/Entertainment	Bride and/or family
Decorations	Bride and/or family
Photographer	Bride and/or family
Videographer	Bride and/or family
Florist	Bride's family pays for ceremony and reception arrangements and bridesmaid's bouquets; Groom's family pays for bride's bouquet, boutonnieres for men, and corsages for mothers and grandmothers

Expense	Responsibility
Marriage license	Groom and/or family
Attendant's Accommodations	Attendants (or bride's family for bridesmaids, groom's family for groomsmen)
Attendants' clothing	Attendants (bridesmaids for dresses, groomsmen for tux rental/purchase)
Honeymoon	Groom and/or family

The (Expensive) Elephant in the Room

So in the real world where etiquette books are great in theory but sometimes challenging in practice, who *really* pays for what? Unfortunately, even in our enlightened, progressive world, most of the time the bride's family will take on the burden of wedding expenses, even beyond what the preceding chart illustrates. So, unless you wish to be thought of as a stingy, stooge-like dad, expect to donate a whole lot to the cause.

As far as your (sort of) future in-laws are concerned, do not expect the groom's family to offer to pay any of these individual expenses, even those expenses they're expected to pay by formal etiquette. It would be wonderful if they picked up the final flower bill, but there's a decent chance they may not. You and your family may decide you don't want their help, anyway … particularly if you suspect it comes with certain expectations or the flexing of decision-making muscle. In the end, a few thousand bucks may not be worth the conflict and stress of having too many cooks in the kitchen. If you feel this way, and would rather handle the expenses yourselves, it is your prerogative to decline their offer to help.

Of course, you'll have to meet with them and discuss the wedding plans before any decisions about who's paying what can be made. If you live in the same general region as the groom's family, etiquette dictates that they should extend an invitation to you. Again, with the traditional rules of etiquette loosening, the bride and groom can also arrange this meeting, or you may even extend the invitation yourself.

Remember, these people are about to become a vital part of your daughter's life, as well as a peripheral part of yours, so it's a good idea to begin cordial relations early. Even if you find you don't "click," their contact with you will not end with the orchestra's last wedding note; you'll be seeing them at every big event in your future grandchildren's lives—like birthdays, graduations, special events, and much more.

If they live out of town, try to coordinate a meeting in advance of the wedding day. You may wish to invite them to your town, particularly if the wedding will take place there, to show them around. If your daughter and future son-in-law live elsewhere, perhaps they can arrange a parents' weekend at their place. Having the kids around as a buffer during the first meeting is definitely a good idea.

 Father Figures

> So will you be Scrooge or Sugar Daddy? Examine your financial situation honestly and discuss it openly as a family. Offer what you can, and don't feel guilty about what you can't. Weddings are beautiful no matter what their final price tags.

This first meeting among the families may or may not include a discussion of wedding finances. For the record, etiquette dictates that the bride's family should not bring up the topic of wedding costs with the groom's family, but rather that you should wait for them to bring it up. After the groom's family has brought up costs, it becomes perfectly acceptable topic to discuss (don't you just love etiquette?). That means if you've eaten a full meal together, shared after-dinner aperitifs and they're halfway out the door without addressing cash flow, it's safe to assume that they will contribute nothing. Go with this assumption until you are informed to the contrary.

What about contributions from the bride and groom? Again, you may wish to decline any offers from them. On the other hand, it may be a financial necessity to accept them, particularly if they're planning a very expensive or large wedding. Keep in mind that they may truly want to contribute, especially if they are financially solvent. Try to discuss the topic openly and honestly as a family, and don't let pride allow you to bite off more wedding cake than you can chew. Though it's an important day in your daughter's life, in the end it *is* just a big party. One fewer ice sculpture isn't going to ruin the marriage or get in the way of the guests' good time.

You may be considering sharing the costs with the bride and groom or the groom's family, but you're just not sure how. There are a number of ways to approach this quandary. If the groom's family asks you what they can pay for, for instance, you may tell them to cover the costs of a certain item, such as the bar, or the flowers, or the band. You could also offer to split the cost of the reception with them 50/50 (or in another percentage you feel comfortable with) or go with the traditional etiquette outlined above. Following proper etiquette makes any situation less awkward, including this one. If all three parties—your family, the groom's family, and the bride and groom as a couple—will share the cost of the wedding, plan ahead what the breakdown will be. For example, your family may cover the cost of the reception food, the groom's family may cover the reception bar, and the bride and groom may cover the cost of clothing, the band, the flowers, and decorations.

Wedding Styles

By now you're probably thinking enough with the diplomacy, just what is this thing really going to cost me? As with any big financial purchase, that depends. There are many factors that contribute to how little or how much you'll pay for this shindig. It's kind of like buying a Ford versus a Ferrari: They'll both eventually get you to the same destination, but the two journeys will differ dramatically.

It all begins with the style of reception your daughter has in mind. The style will be dictated by a number of factors, including the following:

- Size. Will there be 50 guests or 350?
- Time of day. Breakfast, lunch, or dinner?
- Level of formality. Casual, semi-formal, or formal?
- Location. Manhattan or Mobile?
- Style. Cocktails and hors d'oeuvres? Cake and punch? Or a full five-course meal?
- Alternative wedding. Theme wedding? Destination wedding? Weekend wedding?

These factors make it immediately obvious how wedding costs can range from reasonable to incredibly high. However, they can also be "mixed and matched" to fit your budget. For example, if your daughter's heart is set on a formal five-course dinner reception, you may limit the number of guests to offset the high cost of the food. Conversely, if she can't live without inviting 400 of your closest friends and family members, you may wish to consider a cocktails-only reception or a breakfast or lunch reception, which can be significantly less expensive than a dinner reception. (See Chapter 5 for more in-depth strategies on cutting wedding costs.)

> **Dad's Definitions**
>
> A **destination wedding** is a celebration at a chosen location away from home (European and tropical locations are popular), at which the bride and groom marry surrounded by a small group of close family members and friends. A **weekend wedding** consists of weekend-long events for guests beyond the wedding and reception, which may include meals, sporting events, or other get-togethers.

Because wedding costs can vary so much, this book will present average wedding costs for the most popular type of wedding—an evening reception with approximately 180 guests. The costs associated with this "average" wedding are also averaged on a national basis; costs range by region. For instance, if you live in the New York Metro region you should expect to shell out a lot more than the national average, for a total of about $10,000 more for similar quality services and product.

Invitations, thank you notes, etc:	$375-$450
Flowers:	$775-$1,800
Photography/Videography:	$1,200-$1,500
Music:	$750-$1,000
Ceremony fees:	$150-$250
Limousine:	$300-$425
Attendants' gifts:	$300
Wedding rings:	$1,000-$1,800
Engagement ring:	$3,000
Pre-wedding parties:	$600
Bridal attire:	$1,000
Groom's formalwear:	$100
Reception	$5,500-$7,500
Wedding cake:	$300
Wedding favors:	$250
Decorations:	$600
Total:	$16,200-$20,875

I stress again that these prices are *average*. Obviously, you can spend a great deal more on each and every one of these line items, from the ring to the photography. You can also spend less if you use a little resourcefulness and some extra elbow grease. However, these costs offer a benchmark at which to set your expectations—and measure yourselves against—as you continue along in your wedding planning.

Types of Weddings

You've heard the terms "black tie," "black tie optional," "formal," "semi-formal," and "casual" weddings, but what do they entail and how do they compare?

And why do you need to know all this stuff? It's important to understand that the level of formality is usually a significant driver of price; the more formal the wedding, the more expensive it will be. The following is a breakdown of what to expect at each level.

Very formal: The most obvious mark of a very formal wedding is what guests wear. "White tie," means a jacket with tails for men, and full-length gowns for women. The bride would typically be outfitted in a very dramatic gown with a long train and a long veil; the rule goes that the longer the train, the more formal the wedding. Unless you've grown up in Manhattan society attending benefits, parties and charity balls, chances are you and yours have seldom, if ever, attended a white tie event. White tie denotes the crème-de-la-crème of weddings, meaning the food, bar, decorations, and music had better follow in dramatic suit. Ante up.

Formal: Much more common than white tie weddings, "black tie" events mean tuxedos for the men (or a solid dark suit) and full-length or cocktail-length dresses for the women. You've probably attended more than a few black tie events and weddings in your day. These events generally offer a live band, such as an orchestra or swing band; an elegant venue, such as a ballroom, club, or historical site; dramatic tables with beautiful place settings, centerpieces and/or candlelight; top shelf liquor; and a multicourse, sit-down meal.

Semi-formal or casual: Growing in popularity, semi-formal or casual weddings forgo the traditional pomp of formal weddings in favor of a more relaxed attitude. At a less formal wedding, the bride can dress more comfortably, perhaps in a wedding dress with no train, or an off the rack white dress from a decent retailer that she might even be able to wear again. The groom may don a suit or even a sport jacket and pants look. Semi-formal weddings may or may not include a seated meal (a buffet or food stations will do just as nicely), and may include music from a live band or a professional disc jockey. Table settings may be less formal and more frivolous, with colored linens, unusual centerpieces, and other creative touches. And the reception itself may be less structured, with more impromptu toasts, speeches, dances, and mingling.

Deciding on the level of formality of the wedding will set the tone for the rest of your decision-making, easing wedding day choices such as venue, menu, music, décor, and dress. How to choose this level? There's a good chance your daughter has already envisioned this little detail; talk with her and weigh the pros and cons of each before settling on one style. She may not be comfortable in the spotlight and wish to throw as casual a party as possible or she may have always envisioned being princess for a day and nothing less will do. We'll leave this all-important conversation to you, dad.

Setting the Budget

So you've braved the muddy, moody waters of your daughter's wedding desires and you finally have an idea of what she's envisioning. Now you need to set a budget. If you have generously offered to foot the bill, setting an overall budgetary figure is highly advised. Chances are the actual costs will still come in way over budget, but at least the idea of carte blanche will be foiled from the start. But how should you set this all-important figure?

First use the national averages depicted earlier in this chapter to get a ballpark feel for what items like invitations or flowers actually cost. Then, base your own budget on those figures, deciding to either pad them (lucky daughter) or whittle them down. Add the cost of each item and presto! you have an overall figure. Pretty simple stuff.

Paternal Precautions

Expect to go over budget. Between unanticipated or hidden costs and inevitable emotion-based decisions, this party is likely to go well over your original figure. You may even wish to set up a contingency plan, such as your daughter pays half of any expenses that go over budget.

You will inevitably be pressured to up these individual figures. Your daughter will have conversations with people like the caterer and florist who will be selling at all times, promoting the notion that the $20 bottles of wine are *okay*, but *her* wedding is really much more worthy of the $40 bottles. (After all, what will people *think*?) Even if the pressure is not quite so blatant, the rules of sales always apply. Like shopping for, say, a television, even if you walk in intending to buy the 28-inch model, that 36-incher across the aisle sure does tempt you. Your daughter will be similarly lured by things like a sumptuous cocktail hour raw bar and imported flowers from the tropics.

This desire, of course, is a combination of the vendors' seasoned sales techniques and your daughter's inflated expectations. If you work together with your daughter to set an initial budget, and revisit that budget a few times before the wedding date to determine if it's realistic, there will be fewer surprises—and heartache—when it comes to settling the big day's final details.

The Least You Need to Know

- The rules of etiquette continue to change, even when it comes to wedding spending.
- How much you spend for the wedding will depend on where you live.
- Choosing a wedding style will help determine your budget.
- Work together with your daughter to set and keep to a budget.

5

I Think, Therefore I Save

In This Chapter

- Overall strategies for saving money
- Cutting ceremony costs
- Bargain bridal wear
- Containing costs for the reception

We know you, dad. And we know your philosophy. (By "we" I speak for daughters across the world.) It goes something along the line of: "Why spend a dollar when you can spend fifty cents?" and "Nothing's worth buying if it isn't on sale." This theory of spending rings especially true when the purchases do not concern hardware, electronic gadgets and/or accessories for your boat. On this grand scale, wedding flowers just don't make the cut.

But while you may know exactly where to find that bargain basement riding lawnmower, knowing where to find fresh, discounted flowers may be a true mystery to you. And knowing how much is too much to spend is impossible. After all, there's no *Consumer Reports* comparing shelf life, price, and tendency to wilt among species and florists. In other words, weddings involve a highly emotional decision-making—and spending—process, one that's based less on price than it is on sheer aesthetics.

When it comes to weddings, lowest price does not dictate best choice, not by a long shot. However, there are lots of ways that you and your family can cut back and save money. These strategies can serve to reduce your bottom line or free up some of the budget for splurges in other areas of your wedding planning.

Cost-Cutting Lines of Attack

Before you and your daughter begin to search out vendors, there are certain "big-picture" strategies to keep in mind when planning the wedding. These lines of attack are meant to assist you in getting the best price and to protect you from unscrupulous or unprofessional service providers.

- Never mention the word "wedding" when calling caterers, vendors, or other service providers. For many "professionals," this word will result in quoting a significantly higher price than for a conventional party. These vendors know that planning a wedding can be a very emotional process, and that demand outstrips supply if a bride's got her heart set on only one option. They also know that, as a rule, the budget for a wedding outweighs, say, the budget for an anniversary party. So keep your cards close to the vest until the chips are played out, or at least until they quote you for a standard "party."

Paternal Precautions

When calling sites and vendors for initial quotes, avoid mentioning that the party is a wedding, at least until you've got your quote. Vendors have been known to quote 20 to 40 percent more for a wedding than other types of parties.

- Begin planning early. The more time you have, the more you'll be able to shop around and find genuine bargains. The closer the wedding date looms, the more pressure the bride will be under to find a caterer—and a florist and band and limo—quickly. She may be tempted to lock in a vendor before adequately shopping around, and that's no way to find the bargains.

- Decide what the most important aspects of the wedding are and stick to them. If necessary, make a priority list that itemizes each service or thing the bride will be purchasing in order of its importance. Unless there's an unlimited budget, going top-of-the-line for everything is impossible. However, going top-of-the-line in one or two of the most important areas *is* possible if you cut back in other areas to compensate. For example, if your daughter has always dreamed of wearing a designer wedding dress, perhaps you could offset the cost with an alcohol-free wedding (or an hors d'oeuvres only or lunchtime reception). Perhaps you feel that the flower budget would be better used on wedding favors that the guests could take home. By examining your priorities and developing a list ranked by importance, it'll be easier later to avoid the temptations that vendors will inevitably present along the way.

- Pay with a credit card, particularly for deposits. Credit cards offer protection that personal checks and debit cards do not. Just be careful to pay these credit card charges off quickly to avoid adding unnecessary interest payments to your costs.

- Beware of the bait-and-switch. This tactic can (and will) be employed by any type of wedding professional, from musicians to photographers. The bait-and-switch occurs when, say, the wedding photographer you expected sends another in his place. Or half the band members sent to your reception are substitutes for the regular group. Or the chef who cooked your meal for the tasting is off that night. If you want and expect a specific service professional—for any of your services—be sure to get this in writing before you put down your deposit. Also find out what Plan B is for any of these professionals in the event of an emergency.

The Ceremony

When comparing the ceremony and reception, the ceremony is typically the less evil twin when it comes to expenses. At most religious ceremonies, the aesthetics don't have to be created because they're already present in the church or temple or mosque design. Though most brides will factor in some expense for altar flowers, pew bows, an aisle runner, and ceremony music, typically most of the fuss and expense will go toward the reception. The exception to this may be Jewish weddings, at which the chuppah can be very expensive, particularly if extravagantly adorned with fresh flowers.

Of course, there are great ways to save, even on a potentially expensive chuppah. The following sections offer some strategies on how to create a lovely ceremony without breaking the bank.

Officiant's Fee

The officiant's fee is the one line item that's pretty much non-negotiable. It's in very poor taste to negotiate the officiant's fee, which is typically not very high to begin with. Save elsewhere, or have a legally authorized family member or friend perform the ceremony.

Setting

The setting of the wedding can range from a house of worship to your backyard, so it's difficult to estimate the cost of renting space for it. Typically you won't need to pay anything for a religious setting; the cost is often included in the officiant's fee. If the ceremony takes place in a grand building lobby, a hotel ballroom, or another private setting, however, you will need to negotiate price based upon the amount of space you'll need and the amount of time you need it. For a public arena, such as a park, beach or other area, you will most likely need to apply for a permit with the local authorities, usually for a nominal fee. Be sure to check with the municipality in question before you go too far with planning.

Décor

There are many ways to save on ceremony décor. One way is to hold the ceremony in a naturally decorated venue, such as a botanical garden, a rolling waterfront lawn, or a forest clearing, which eliminates the need for elaborate flower arrangements or other décor. Another strategy useful for indoor ceremonies is to piggyback the wedding onto a holiday season. For a Christian wedding, choose a church that's known for its beautiful Christmas or Easter flowers. By planning the ceremony in the weeks surrounding these holidays (Advent or Lent, for example), you'll be able to take advantage of the extra-beautiful surroundings without spending a dime. (This strategy also applies to reception venues, which also deck themselves out for holidays ranging from New Year's Eve to Halloween.)

 Father Figures

A Bridal bouquet can cost well over $100. A bouquet with a single, elegant bloom such as a sunflower or tulip can be just as beautiful and cost a fraction of the price.

Another way to save on ceremony flowers is to find out if there are any other weddings at your site on the same day. For example, if there are two other weddings at your church following your daughter's morning ceremony, she may wish to share the cost of her flower arrangements with the other brides, if they are willing. This common practice can cut the cost of ceremony décor significantly. A third way to save on ceremony décor is the do-it-yourself approach. If there's someone crafty in the family, ask them to make pew bows instead of purchasing expensive, marked-up bows from the florist. You can also create inexpensive wedding programs on a laser or color printer. Use a slightly heavier paper stock to make them more substantial or sandwich them within a heavy colored paper to create a "dust cover."

Music

For both the ceremony and the reception, the fewer the number of musicians, the less expensive your music will be. A duet will be half the cost of a quartet, a soloist a fraction of the cost of a choir, and so on. There are some additional ways to save money on musicians specific to the ceremony. Churches and synagogues typically work with affiliated musicians who may charge less than outside musicians do. Logistically this can help, too, as affiliated musicians are used to working with one another and know the ropes at their particular location. Often an organist or soloist may even be included in the ceremony "donation" or officiant's fee.

You may also call your local college, university, or even high school for recommendations of student musicians. If they do not belong to a union, they will typically cost less than professional musicians, often without any compromise to quality of the music. However, be sure to listen to a tape or live audition first. Or if you have friends or family members who are musicians or vocalists, ask them to perform at your wedding. Not only is it considered an honor, it can also double as your wedding gift.

Clothing and Accessories

Wedding day clothing costs a lot of money, relatively speaking. It's particularly costly if you analyze cost vs. wear (i.e., more than $100 per hour of wear for the average wedding gown). Bridal dresses start at around $500 and go up from there (designer gowns cost about $2000 and up). By comparison, tuxedo rentals are cheap, around $100 or less. You may already own a tuxedo, in which case you'll probably want to wear that or you may feel it's time to purchase a new one, particularly if you believe you'll have occasion to wear it again in the near future.

For the Bride and Women

There aren't many discounts or sales at bridal shops. Chances are that your daughter won't be seeing a President's Day "White Sale" on wedding dresses advertised at any of the local boutiques. Why? Once again, it's the old supply-and-demand routine. Most brides are ready and willing to spend big bucks on this, the most important outfit they'll ever buy. So with few exceptions, bridal shops can command their own prices.

There are, however, a few tricks of the trade when it comes to finding a lower-cost bridal gown. The first and most obvious are "discount" bridal chains. These stores offer brides the ability to buy dresses "off the rack," which means they buy the actual dress they're trying on, rather than ordering a dress based on a sample, as is true with traditional boutiques. Chain bridal stores such as "David's Bridal" carry gowns in many sizes and styles that the bride-to-be can try on and take home all in the same day.

Usually these dresses are less expensive than dresses at most designer shops. Oftentimes discount bridal shops carry "knock-offs" or copies of more expensive designer dresses. And these stores also have sales.

 "Pop"ositions

> Ask your daughter whether she'd like to wear her mother's wedding dress. It can be altered to fit both her and today's styles. Doing so represents another way to save money on the wedding dress.

However, even if your daughter wouldn't be caught dead in a dress that she didn't find on the pages of *Bride Magazine*, you have some options. Most areas of the country have "warehouse" stores that carry designer dresses that can be taken home the same day, at significantly lower prices. The catch is that many brides-to-be may have tried on the dresses, and you have to buy the dress in the condition in which you find it (again, the bride won't be ordering a brand new one). The selection may also be a bit more random, but who said finding bargains is easy?

Another great way to find a designer dress at a lower price is to scout out traditional bridal boutiques for clearance sales. These sales typically feature dresses that are a few seasons old and have been discontinued by the dressmaker. The catch is finding a sample that fits, both in size and in style. However, by regularly scouting out these bridal shops, your daughter may eventually find a designer dress for a real bargain.

Another method of finding bridal gowns at a discount is on the Internet. Shoppers willing to do a little legwork can find virtually any style gown, and even specific designer styles can be found and purchased at a discount. If your daughter has found the gown she can't live without in a bridal magazine, for instance, she should be able to find it cheaper through an Internet site than through a traditional bridal shop. Advise her to start with www.theknot.com to find dresses; a simple search for "discount wedding dresses" will also yield hundreds of links.

Your daughter may be able to find an even better bargain if she's willing to wear a pre-worn dress that she's purchased or rented. If she has enough time, your daughter may find her dream dress at a consignment shop, in a classified ad, or at a rental shop. These gowns have probably only been worn once (or in some cases, not at all) and are cleaned for resale. If your daughter has time and patience (and shares your frugal attitude), she might be able to find a designer dress for a fraction of the price. To find these potential gems, look through your local newspaper, visit reputable consignment shops in nicer areas of town, or look up rental gowns in your yellow pages. These strategies can also be an ideal way to find nontraditional wedding dresses, or period costumes, if your daughter is having a special theme wedding.

Pre-worn (and new) wedding dresses are also available at www.ebay.com, the immensely popular online auctioneer, where virtually every type of good and service is available. Gowns range in style and price, and you can find a beautiful traditional wedding gown for under $100. Also available are veils, gloves, and other accessories. E-bay offers perhaps the widest selection of pre-worn dresses you'll find anywhere.

Mother of the Bride

The mother of the bride can also use most of the strategies outlined for the bride when it comes to finding her dress. Discount stores like David's Bridal carry traditional mother of the bride dresses, as do bridal shops (usually at a higher price than the discount stores.) Depending on how formal she'd like to dress, a mother has a bit more flexibility. She can shop at finer department stores and specialty boutiques for dresses that may not be official "mother of the bride" dresses (at official mother of the bride prices).

For the Groom and Gentlemen

Compared to women's outfits, men's wedding clothing is relatively simple. The biggest decision you and the groom will have to make is whether to buy or to rent, a decision ultimately based on price and practicality. If the wedding will be black tie, the groom, groomsmen, you, and the groom's father will be donning tuxedos, with bow ties and vests or cummerbunds in the color and style of the groom's choosing. If you have a tuxedo (that fits) already, talk to the groom about the possibility of wearing it; the one you own is probably of better quality and fit than one you could rent. If you don't own one, the groom will undoubtedly make rental arrangements at a local tuxedo shop. Often these shops compete with each other by offering special deals and discounts, so advise your future son-in-law to shop around and keep his eyes open for special promotions. He or your daughter may ask you to wear a particular color or style in accessories, so be prepared to buy or rent part of your outfit.

Paternal Precautions

Be sure to try on the suit you plan to wear in plenty of time before the wedding. You'll need the extra time to get it cleaned, altered—or to buy a new one, if necessary.

If your daughter is not having a black tie wedding, a suit may be a more appropriate choice of evening (or day) wear. This is a good time to spring for a new suit, especially if you haven't recently purchased one. It might be a good idea to take your wife, daughter, or significant other along for advice, and go to a shop that alters the suit if necessary. Purchase a good-quality suit, shirt, tie, and shoes. You're hosting your daughter's wedding, after all, and there's no better occasion to look your spiffiest. For specific styles and trends in men's formalwear, see Chapter 6.

The Reception

The reception is generally where you'll spend the big bucks. The bad news is that unless you want to do it yourself completely, you better plan on shelling out more dough that you'd like. The good news is that you can have a tasteful, elegant affair without completely breaking the bank.

The most important caveat to remember when budgeting for the reception is the more guests you invite, the more expensive the wedding will be. You may have heard talk of a "per-head" cost—this is the cost of the reception, with everything from food to alcohol to entertainment factored in and divided by the number of guests. It's usually referred to as a basis for gift-giving. There's a common perception that guests are supposed to give a gift that equals the "per-head" cost of the wedding. (This is actually a misperception—guests should give gifts in an amount that they can afford or want to give.) In any case, the cost of the wedding increases in direct proportion to the number of guests. If you'd like to put a cap on costs, you can first put a cap on the number of guests.

If this simply is not possible, then you'll need to cut in other areas, such as in the amount or type of food or alcohol. The following sections offer cost-saving strategies for various areas of the wedding.

The Right Space/Site

The most obvious way to save on the cost of a site rental is to host the wedding at home. But because space limitations may make this a logistical nightmare for most families, we'll focus on finding bargains *outside* your backyard.

Time may be your best ally in finding wedding site bargains. The further ahead you're able to plan, the better consumer you'll be, as you'll be in a position to compare prices and make more informed choices. Also, by booking the reception a year or more ahead of time, you'll be in a better position to negotiate price.

You should also consider hosting the wedding on a day other than Saturday, which is most in demand (particularly in the spring and summer months.) By having the wedding on a Friday or Sunday, for instance, the space may be available at a reduced rate, and caterers, florists, photographers, and musicians may also charge below their normal Saturday rates.

Thinking "out of the box" may also yield a less expensive venue. To marry in a public park, for instance, you'll probably need to pay for little besides a permit. Keep in mind, however, that non-traditional venues will require rental of everything from tables to chairs to dishware and cutlery, which can end up costing more than a traditional catering hall or restaurant. Beware the hidden costs.

Eat and Be Merry

Saving money on wedding reception food is as common sense as saving money when you go out for a meal: Don't order the surf-and-turf, skip the appetizers, and don't even think about wine or cocktails.

While these caveats ring true, you also don't want to go underboard when you're hosting a festive affair for your closest family and friends. If you're inviting guests from near and far, you'll want to give them something special to remember and something to celebrate. It is possible to host a pleasing affair while keeping costs in check.

For instance, instead of serving butler-passed hors d'oeuvres during the cocktail hour, set up a spread of veggies and cheeses. This relatively simple but satisfying offering will quiet pre-dinner stomach grumbles and will prevent cocktails from going straight to guests' heads.

When it comes to the main course, any dish the caterer prepares should be satisfying and aesthetically pleasing, whether it's the filet mignon or the roasted chicken. Don't feel pressured to choose the most expensive item on the catering menu, and don't feel you have to serve multiple courses. While a five-course meal is certainly elegant, a three-course meal consisting of a pre-dinner salad or soup, main course, and post-dinner dessert will satisfy all but the snootiest crowd.

Probably the most significant way to save money on the reception (besides cutting the guest list) is to serve lunch or brunch instead of dinner, which is typically much less expensive at most venues. Obviously you'll need to plan a morning or very-early afternoon ceremony, immediately followed by the reception.

Some brides and grooms also opt to throw hors d'oeuvres-only affairs, with no dinner. If it's an evening wedding, be sure to let guests know in advance that dinner will not be served, lest they arrive starving. And serve plenty of hors d'oeuvres to offset the effects of any alcohol served.

Finally, if your caterer allows it (and many will not) arrange for a homemade dessert buffet to be offered with coffee service. As a wedding gift, ask some close friends and family members to donate their favorite sweet for everyone to enjoy as a late-party snack.

Toasting with Style

There's one foolproof way to save on the cost of reception alcohol—don't serve it. But when it comes to celebrating, this option may not be one you care to explore.

Unfortunately alcohol can cost almost as much—and sometimes more, depending on the details—as the food. There are a number of plans popularly offered by caterers, including the "per-bottle" spending plan, for which you'll be required to pay for only what is consumed and the "per-head" plan, for which you'll pay a certain amount per-head per hour whether the guest is drinking pale ale or ginger ale. The general rule goes that if you've got a heavy drinking crowd, the per-head, per-hour plan is probably the route to take; if you believe there will be light drinking, go with the per-bottle arrangement.

Paternal Precautions

If you're paying for alcohol per bottle, beware of unscrupulous caterers. You may even wish to view and count the empty bottles yourself at the end of the night, to be sure that they've provided you with an accurate charge.

Whether you go with the per-head or per-bottle plan, there are number of other ways to pay less for alcohol. The first is to offer a wine-and-beer only bar. While some guests may grumble if they can't order their favorite cocktail, it can save on the cost of the bar significantly, even if you serve good quality wines and beer.

Another method to save is to forgo serving "top shelf" liquor for less expensive liquor. Top shelf liquor typically includes the more exclusive, expensive brands such as imported beers and high-end spirits. Again, drinking snobs may turn up their noses to a lower shelf offering, but they're not paying the bill. If you'd like to compromise, caterers usually offer a middle-tier quality alcohol that's not the best, but certainly is not the worst.

Some more tips on saving money:

- Do not open the bar until after dinner. Serve punch or wine only during the cocktail hour and meal.

- Close the bar an hour before the reception ends and provide soft drinks and coffee.

- If it's allowed, bring your own bar. Buy cases of liquor, wine, beer and mixers, and hire a bartender to serve. Keep in mind you will also need to furnish glasses, garnishes, and other bar staples. Return any unopened bottles for a refund.

Conducting the Music

The general rule for reception music is that a DJ is less expensive than a band, and a small band is less expensive than a larger band. This rule is based on a simple premise: You pay for man-hours, so the more people you're hiring, the more expensive it will be. Ask if a favorite band performs with fewer members. Many bands are flexible: A 10-piece orchestra, for instance, may have an auxiliary group that performs with just 5 or 6 members of the band who charge a lower rate.

Although there's no substitute for live music, a quality DJ can be just as effective in getting the crowd on the dance floor. In fact, some people prefer to dance to their familiar favorites rather than to new renditions of popular tunes.

Obviously, whether you choose live or taped music is a matter of preference and budget. Before making either choice, however, be sure to shop around and listen to what the musicians/DJ have to offer before you book them. A DJ who's obnoxious as master of ceremonies is no bargain, even if he does charge a hundred dollars less than the next guy. You want your guests to remember the wedding, not the DJ.

Another way to cut costs of the music is to cut the amount of time they play. Instead of hiring the band to perform for five hours, hire them for three (though you should beware of minimum time clauses).

 Father Figures

When hiring a band, think flexibly and communicate with the band members. If your budget is lower than their asking price, negotiate for fewer band members or a slightly shorter performance. If the wedding takes place on an off-day like Sunday, they may rather charge a cut-rate than have no gig at all.

Choosing the Décor

The décor, including flowers, provides the most flexible area in which to save money on your wedding. The more creative you are, the more you can save. And the more you can do yourself, the higher the margin of savings.

Fresh flowers are very expensive, there's no way around it. However, there are immediate and swift methods to reduce the flower bill right off the bat. First of all, choose blooms that are in season. Out of season flowers require special shipping from regions where they *are* in season, making them difficult to come by, and thus more expensive. In addition, some flowers inherently are more expensive than others; wildflowers, for instance, will often be less expensive than long-stem roses. Often silk flowers—or a silk and live flower mix—will cost less than all fresh flower bouquets or centerpieces.

Finally, the bride is not limited to floral centerpieces. More and more brides are choosing creative centerpieces ranging from flowering plants or balloon arrangements to candle arrangements or seasonal-theme centerpieces. By no means is the bride strictly limited to the traditional elaborate rose centerpiece—and, cost aside, she may decide to choose something more personal or unique.

Father Figures _____

> To save money and include a personal
> touch, the bride may wish to borrow vases
> and flower holders from friends and family
> members to use as centerpieces. Often the
> florist's mark-up on simple glass vases
> alone can be astronomical. Buying vases
> in bulk at a craft shop is another option.

Let Them Eat Cake

Currently, the average cost for a wedding cake is
$3 a slice. That means if you have 150 guests, the
average cost for the entire cake is $450; for 250
guests it's a whopping $750. And that's the average.
Cakes can cost much more.

Fortunately, there are methods to save on the wedding cake. Certain styles and designs are more
expensive than others right off the bat. A fondant
style cake, for instance, is more time-consuming to
prepare and thus more expensive than a butter
cream cake. In general, the more elaborate the
cake, the more expensive it will be.

If your daughter's heart is set on a fantasy fondant
wedding cake, all hope is not lost. One trick of the
wedding trade is to go with your desired cake
design but in a much smaller size. When dessert
time comes, the caterer should slice and serve the
cake from inside the kitchen, supplementing it with
specially baked sheet cakes in the same flavor.

Doing so can save you, on average, about $2.50 a slice. And your guests will never know the difference.

Another strategy when serving dessert is to limit this course to cake only, instead of serving a caterer-prepared dessert *and* a wedding cake. If you feel wedding cake isn't quite enough, serve a scoop of ice cream on the side, or get a special flavored cake like cheesecake for a more substantial dessert.

Picture Perfect

As with the cost of musicians, it's difficult to be completely frugal about the photographer, as good quality goes a long way. The worst-case scenario is the photographer who doesn't show up; the second worst-case is the one who takes bad pictures. There's no way to be adequately reimbursed for poor results—you can't go back and photograph those moments again.

In other words, don't scrimp on the photographer to save a few bucks. That doesn't mean you have to hire the most expensive photographer, however. Ask around for recommendations and be sure to view a number of photographers' portfolios before booking one. Also, be sure if you're booking with a studio that you are hiring who you think you're hiring. Some studios pull the old bait-and-switch, where you think you've hired one photographer until his inexperienced assistant shows up to handle the wedding. Be sure to get specifics in writing.

Paternal Precautions

Yes, the quality and cost of the photographer is important. But so is his/her personality. Be sure you find a professional you feel compatible with, or be prepared to be irritated by him or her throughout your daughter's wedding day.

Another way to limit the photographer's cost is to limit the amount of time he or she works the wedding and reception. Once again, the longer the photographer is required to shoot photos, the more expensive the price. Compare studio and photographer prices and ask about different packages. Even if the photographer leaves before the reception ends, you can still get a record of the later moments by asking friends or family members to take photos with cameras you provide (disposable or otherwise.)

Do Me a Favor

Wedding favors, those little tchotchkes given to guests as special mementos, are certainly not required, but can provide a nice personal touch. Of course, the least expensive favor is the one that isn't there. There is certainly a contingent that believes wedding favors are unnecessary and often overlooked or tossed away by guests. But, if the bride has her heart set on including wedding favors, there are a couple of ways she can cut costs:

- The do-it-herself approach. Instead of purchasing high-priced items, she (along with
  help from her bridesmaids or family, may
  choose to make or assemble something herself. For example, if she'd like to give out
  miniature boxes of chocolates, it will be
  cheaper to buy the candy and the chocolate
  both in bulk, and then fill and decorate the
  boxes by hand. Other ideas include giving
  out mini-dried flower arrangements, hand-
  made bookmarks, little boxed soaps, or a
  tiny vase with a single flower bud, which
  double as part of the table décor.

Dad's Definitions

A **wedding favor** is a small gift that's
given to your wedding guests. Commonly-
given favors are candy, small picture
frames (which double as place card hold-
ers), or flowers.

- The bargain basement approach. There's no
  better place to find wedding bargains than
  the Internet, and favors are no exception. A
  simple search for "wedding favors" on the
  web yields thousands of sites. Check out
  these sites for closeout sales, and compare
  prices with traditional retail vendors before
  purchasing.

Just When You Thought It Was Over ...

No, it's not over yet. There are other nonreception-related expenses you may also incur during your planning—and more opportunities to save money.

Wedding Pre-Parties

If you decide to throw an engagement party (or find yourselves footing the bill for the rehearsal dinner), there are no rules that dictate how you should do it. These parties are much more flexible than the wedding or reception, which, as you've discovered, have many more "must-have" expenses such as cake, music, and a full meal.

Engagement parties, however, are simply a chance to celebrate the impending nuptials of the happy couple and have far fewer rules. There are a number of easy ways to keep the cost of an engagement party or rehearsal dinner low.

- Have it at home. Even if you have catering help with food or alcohol, you will save money by throwing the party at home rather than at a restaurant or hall.

- Throw a cocktail party. A party doesn't have to include a meal. Throw the party after (or before) the dinner hour, and include cocktails and hors d'oeuvres only.

- Host a different meal. Throw a luncheon or brunch party, which can be significantly less expensive than dinner.
- Keep it casual. Host a backyard barbecue or pool party, rather than a dressy affair with expensive food and drink.

Invitations

Invitations can be another surprisingly high expense for the wedding, especially if the bride insists upon certain conventions, such as engraving and calligraphy. However, there are equally elegant alternatives that save you 40 percent or more compared to formal engraved invitations.

One option is buying invitations made using a technique called thermography. Thermography results in a raised-letter, embossed effect similar to engraving, at a much lower price point.

 Father Figures

> The cost of postage is easily over-looked. Obviously, the heavier the invitation, the more expensive it will be to mail. Remember to figure in the cost of postage when choosing the invitation and inserts. The stationer should be able to give some postage estimates.

You can request the thermography technique from your local print source or through online vendors.

Internet invitation sites offer additional savings by selling you invitations direct, with countless styles and options. Again, it's as easy to find wedding invitations online as it is to find favors; simply type "wedding invitations" into your search engine and you'll find hundreds of sites to browse. Compare prices to those offered by your local stationer or bridal boutique; most likely invitations will be much less expensive if purchased over the Internet.

Of course, you can always make your own invitations with a computer and a printer. Keep in mind that the print quality is not nearly as elegant as that of a traditional printer, but if you have a little design sense and a decent-quality printer, many guests will hardly notice. Buy high-quality paper and make sure you've got plenty of ink or use a laser printer for crisper print quality.

Transportation

The bride and groom shouldn't have to drive themselves around on their wedding day, but there are alternatives to the traditional limousine service. If you do go with a limo, be sure to shop around and choose a reputable company; again, it won't matter how cheap the service is if it doesn't show up.

 "Pop"ositions

If you have a friend or family member with a great classic car, ask them to loan it or rent it to you for a day.

For an alternative to the traditional limo, you may wish to rent a luxury car and appoint someone to be chauffeur—cars like a Lincoln Town Car, Jaguar, or Cadillac are perfect and may be a relatively inexpensive one-day rentals, at least compared to hiring a limo. If you need to transport many guests, look into a minibus or a trolley, which are less expensive alternatives to renting multiple limousines.

The Honeymoon

The cost and planning of the honeymoon are by no means your responsibility, but some brides' parents have been known to pay for the honeymoon as a wedding gift (I know, I know, isn't the wedding itself gift enough?). If you do find you have room for a honeymoon in your budget, there are also ways to get a great deal:

- The Internet is your friend. There are countless sites devoted to travel planning on the Internet, and many cater to discount travel. Check out sites like www.orbitz.com or www.travelocity.com to find great deals on package vacations, cruises, hotels, rental cars, and flights, often at rates much lower than a travel agents'.

- Wait until the last minute. If your daughter and her husband are delaying their honeymoon for strictly financial reasons, why not surprise them with an all-expenses paid trip—that you've paid for? Often Internet or travel agents' best deals come with last-minute bookings (cruises or all-inclusive resorts are a good example). Try to give them a little advance notice, though, so the bride and groom can tie up any loose ends at work or fulfill other obligations.

The Least You Need to Know

- It is possible to cut costs without cutting quality.
- Wait to tell vendors that you're planning a wedding until you get a firm price for the services he or she offers.
- The more you can do yourselves—from designing and printing invitations to hosting a pre-wedding party at your home—the more you can reduce costs.

Chapter 6

Fine Frocks

In This Chapter

- A suit or a tuxedo—which is appropriate?
- Buying vs. renting formalwear
- Styles of formalwear and accessories
- Tips for the perfect shave

Is it ever better to look good than to feel good? Generally not, but when you look your best, you tend to feel your best, too. But where do you start? If the thought of donning formalwear fills you with dread, keep this in mind: It's never as bad as you imagine. And with a few helpful tips, you're sure to come out looking and smelling like a rose.

This chapter covers how to look your best from the inside out, including everything from formalwear options to accessory choices to tips for a spiffy shoe shine. It also includes male-oriented tips for skin care, the perfect shave, and hair care so you'll be in ship-shape for the big day.

Formalwear: To Buy or to Rent?

When it comes to choosing threads for your daughter's wedding, the first big decision you'll need to make is whether you'd prefer to purchase or rent your formalwear. Assuming the wedding is black tie, which means you'll be wearing a tuxedo chosen by the groom, you'll probably have the option to do either. Typically, the groom (often with the bride's help) chooses a style of tuxedo for himself, the groomsmen, his father, and you. However, he may be open to letting you choose your own tuxedo within reason. If you already own a tuxedo, discuss the possibility of wearing it before he begins shopping around. If it's a classic style, he should have no problem with that option. However, if absolute uniformity (i.e., double-breasted, six-button jackets with powder blue shirts) is the bride and groom's goal, you may need to purchase or rent a monkey suit unique to the occasion.

The decision of whether to buy or rent is based solely on price; you'll be able to get the same style whether you rent or buy. Renting will cost about 10 to 30% of the purchase price, but if you know you'll need formalwear for a few more occasions in the near future, and it's a style that suits you (i.e., NOT the powder blue), it may be worth it to purchase your tux. At an average price of $300 to $500, it will have paid for itself in just three to four wears. You may also explore the option of purchasing a used tuxedo from a rental shop. Often rental shops will sell you a full tuxedo for $100 to $150 if it's been pre-worn (Be sure to examine it carefully to ensure it's in good condition.)

Of course, you may prefer to buy a tuxedo simply because you don't like the idea of pre-worn clothing. Rest assured that the vendor cleans them between rentals. However, if you can't stomach the thought of it, buying may be your only option.

Overdressed vs. Underdressed

Of course before you buy or rent anything, it's a good idea to determine what style and level of formality is appropriate. For a semi-formal or formal evening wedding, tuxedos are the optimum choice. Choose a dark or black tuxedo for semi-formal, or a black tuxedo for formal. For a summer wedding or a tropical locale, a white dinner jacket with formal black trousers is also appropriate.

For a semi-formal daytime wedding, go with a suit in navy or charcoal. Khaki, white, or seersucker suits are appropriate for semi-formal summer affairs.

For formal or very formal daytime weddings, tuxedos or gray cutaway coats are appropriate. For an ultra-formal look, don an ascot and vest, or go with a tailcoat with a top hat, spats, and gloves.

Very formal evening weddings demand white tie formalwear, which means a black tailcoat, black trousers, a black vest or cummerbund, and a white bow tie.

Talk to your daughter and the groom to determine the best choice in formalwear. If the occasion is white tie, or they would like you to wear a style you don't think you'll wear again (like a cutaway coat), you'll probably wish to rent rather than buy.

Renting Guidelines

Perhaps you're shopping around with the groom to find a reputable formalwear shop, or your daughter has asked you to do some scouting on their behalf. The following are some factors to consider before choosing a formalwear shop.

"Pop"ositions

If the wedding calls for you to wear a suit rather than a tuxedo, now may be the time to purchase a new one. Take some time to shop around, and purchase from a reputable shop that can do alterations on-site.

- Find out which retailers offer special promotions or deals. For instance, some shops offer a free tux rental for the groom or the bride and groom's fathers if the whole wedding party registers there (bonus!).
- Check out their inventory. Make sure they have a full range of current tuxedo styles and accessory options (vests, cummerbunds, etc.) so you can choose the best style for you.

- Be sure the shop can accommodate everyone, including groomsmen or other parties who live out of town.

- Ask if the cost of alterations is included in the rental price. Also determine what accessories are included. Often a few basic styles of cummerbund or vest are included, but there may be an additional charge for specialty vests or trendier styles.

- Ask how they will accommodate you if a last-minute problem should occur. Do they have a tailor available for emergency alterations?

- Find out their pick-up and return policy.

- Ask about late fees and damage fees.

Once you've decided upon a reputable tuxedo shop, there are a few additional points to remember when renting formalwear:

- Shop early, especially if the wedding will be in spring or early summer. By doing so you'll ensure that the styles you want will still be available—even during prom season, when shops are typically strained for inventory. Be sure to reserve formalwear at least 3 to 4 months in advance.

- Be sure the shop gives you a proper fitting at the time you reserve, including measurements of the inseam, waist, and jacket size.

- Order all the accessories you'll need in advance, including tie, cummerbund, vest, cuff links, and shoes.

- If possible, pick up your formalwear a couple days in advance of the wedding and try it on at the shop. The shop should be able to perform any last-minute alterations at that time as well. This way you'll be sure you have the right tuxedo in the right size and you won't have any surprises the morning of the wedding.

Formalwear Sizing

Follow these tips for ensuring the proper size when renting or purchasing formalwear.

- Shirts should hug the neck and be neither too loose nor too tight. If the shirt size you've worn since college seems a little snug in the neck, it may be time to go up a half size or two. (Sorry, dad.)

- Pants should touch the top of your shoes (Bring along the shoes you plan to wear with your tux for ideal fit).

- Check for side buckles on the waistband; they are often adjustable.

- Jacket should fit snugly but comfortably around the shoulders, with no arm bulges and some room at the waist.

- Jacket collar should hug the neck and lapels shouldn't buckle.

- Jacket sleeves should end at the wrist bone.

It's All about Style

A tux is a tux is a tux, right? Not by a long shot. Certainly men are somewhat more limited than women in their choice of clothing, but there are still a large variety of styles, cuts, and accessories that allow you to exhibit your own personal style. The following jacket styles, shirt styles, and accessories can be mixed and matched to create a look that's uniquely your own. (With the bride and groom's approval, of course ...)

"Pop"ositions _____

If the bride and groom are leaving the next day for their honeymoon, offer to return the tuxes to the rental shop. It'll be one less thing the groom has to worry about, and a nice, fatherly thing to do.

Jacket Styles

- Single-breasted. The single-breasted jacket has one row of buttons down the front, which may include one, two, three, or four buttons. The more buttons you choose, the taller and leaner you should be. Single button jackets are most flattering for men who tend to be a bit thick around the middle because it helps them avoid that stuffed-sausage look.

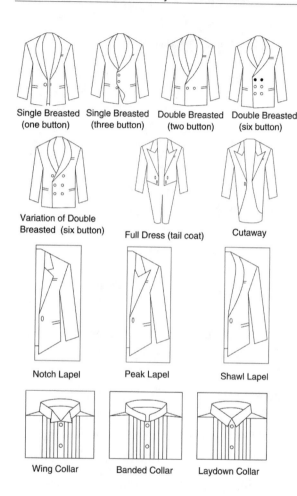

Single Breasted (one button)   Single Breasted (three button)   Double Breasted (two button)   Double Breasted (six button)

Variation of Double Breasted (six button)   Full Dress (tail coat)   Cutaway

Notch Lapel   Peak Lapel   Shawl Lapel

Wing Collar   Banded Collar   Laydown Collar

- Double-breasted. Traditionally, double-breasted jackets appear a bit boxier than single-breasted styles. However, shaped double-breasted jackets have come on the scene in recent years. A double-breasted style is an excellent choice for any body type, as it will help hide a few extra pounds.

- Tailcoats. The most formal of tuxedo jackets, tailcoats are the "mullet haircut" of formalwear—short in front, long in back. Never mullet in style, though, the tailcoat is sharp and appropriate for ultra-formal occasions.

- Cutaway coat (a.k.a. morning coat). This jacket tapers from the waistline button to one broad tail in the back with a vent, and looks great on just about any body type. This style is most appropriate for formal daytime weddings.

- Dinner jacket. This is a single- or double-breasted jacket in white or ivory, meant to be worn with formal black trousers. This style should be worn in warm weather only.

Shoes

Gone are the days when you're required to wear only patent leather pumps or suede slip-ons with your tuxedo. Today, the black leather lace-up shoes you'd wear with a business suit are now perfectly appropriate in the formalwear arena. Be sure your shoes are made of quality, high-grade leather and that they are freshly polished and shined. For a great do-it-yourself shoeshine, follow these tips:

Paternal Precautions _____

Be sure your shoes are in tip-top condition, which means no worn soles and no crescent-shaped heels. If the uppers are still in good condition, have them resoled or reheeled by a shoemaker.

- Place shoes on a sheet of newspaper or other protective surface, and brush off any surface dirt with a paper towel or rag.

- Remove stains with a leather conditioning lotion (available at shoe stores, drug stores, or men's clothing stores).

- Apply a thin layer of appropriately hued polish with a small brush.

- Rub in polish with circular strokes. Wipe off any excess polish.

- Use a second polishing brush to brush the shoe with long strokes, creating a matte finish.

- Buff the shoe with a rag to create a smooth shine.

Accessories

Accessories can take a basic tux and make it sing (and by following some basic style guidelines, it won't be off-key). There are many accessories to choose from to achieve a look that's all your own.

- Vests. There are low vests and there are high vests. High vests, which generally button just around the chest bone, are the hot trend right now, worn by the stylish set in place of either cummerbunds or low vests. If you plan to take off your jacket over the course of the evening, do not go with a low vest, which is typically connected in the back with a single narrow strap and looks tacky if exposed. On the other hand, it's perfectly acceptable to wear a high vest without a jacket. High vests generally look better on taller, narrowly built men. If you're broad-chested, choose a muted color over a bright hue. In fact, a muted, solid color vest is never a bad decision.

- Cummerbund. A cummerbund is the wide band of fabric you wear across your waist and fasten in the back, and it is an alternative to the vest (you wouldn't wear both together.) At most tux shops, cummerbunds are available in a vast range of colors; the bride and groom may choose a color that complements the bridesmaids' dresses. A black cummerbund is always classic and classy.

Paternal Precautions

When choosing accessories, less is always more. Less color, fewer frills, and fewer patterns will always look classic and elegant, never loud or tacky.

- Shirts. Typically your tux rental shop will offer a standard, white wing-collar shirt as part of the package. You may be able to choose the shirt that best suits your style to rent or purchase. In addition to the wing-collar style, which you should wear with a bow tie or ascot (never a long tie), you can also wear a lay-down, or spread collar, shirt. Lay-down collars can be worn with either a bow tie or a long tie. As for shirt color, you can never go wrong with white, and when you look back at the pictures in a few years, you'll be glad you did.

- Ties. The bow tie is classic, always in style, and they come in many colors and patterns at most tux shops. For an elegant black tie look, go with black; for an ultra-formal wedding, white tie is the way to go. An alternative to the bow tie, and very trendy right now among Hollywood types, is the classic long tie worn with a lay-down collar shirt. Your best choice is a black tie with a high sheen for a more formal look; don't even think about wearing that old red-and-blue presidential tie you're so fond of.

- Studs and cufflinks. The choice of whether or not to wear studs over your shirt buttons is yours, but they certainly make an elegant statement. If you opt for them, choose a classic, understated style in the proper size. Hot right now in both studs and cuff links is silver, which provides a sharp-looking complement to many of today's popular accessory styles, such as silver-toned vests and cummerbunds. You may own a special set of cufflinks and studs; if not, take this opportunity to buy some you'll have forever.

Beyond Threads

Of course, there's more to looking good than a snazzy suit. As your daughter or wife can attest from years of experience, it takes a certain amount of effort for your hair and skin to look healthy and vibrant; for your body to be in top shape; and for your hands and nails to look clean and neat. And while this all may be too much effort for the off-season (i.e., after the wedding), looking your best for your daughter's day will be well worth the extra work, especially when all eyes are upon you as you deliver your toast. Let's start with your face and work our way down.

A Proper Shave

A good shave that prevents razor burn or rash is probably something you've been working on for many years now, with some degree of success. If you haven't quite perfected it, however, the following tips will help you achieve a quality shave. Practice following these guidelines a few times before the wedding so you'll get it just right.

- Before shaving, exfoliate. "Exfoliating" is sloughing off dead skin to make new, healthy skin glow, and there are various products on the market that will help you. Ask your wife or daughter for their advice. Chances are they probably have one or two exfoliating products in their beauty bags already. Typically, you massage the exfoliating lotion into your skin and rinse. You'll open your pores and remove dry, flaky skin, creating a perfect canvas for your upcoming shave.

 Father Figures

> A razor stored in a small bath of vodka can stay sharp up to 3 times longer than one stored in the open air. And with all that money you're spending on the wedding, it can't hurt to save a little money on those oh-so-expensive razors …

- Douse your skin with plenty of warm water before shaving to open pores and soften facial hair, lessening irritation and razor burn. If you shower before you shave, the steam and water from that activity can help achieve sufficiently wet, warm skin.

- Thoroughly massage shaving cream into skin, which will allow the cream to better moisturize and take hold of stubble before you run your razor across it.

- Use a fresh blade. Dull, old blades are more apt to cause nicks and irritate the skin because you'll have to use more pressure to cut the hair.

- Rinse your blade often. Don't allow shaving cream and stubble to build up on the blade.

- Use slow, short strokes so that you'll have greater control over the area you're shaving, and thus create less irritation.

- Shave with the grain, which is the direction that the hair naturally grows. When you shave in the opposite direction of hair growth, it causes irritation and the inevitable razor burn or nicked skin.

- Use moisturizer when you are finished shaving. You'll be amazed at how much better your skin will appear over time with the simple application of hydrating moisturizer, giving your skin more elasticity and a healthier-looking tone. Raid your wife or daughter's medicine cabinet, or buy a moisturizer especially suited for men at a drug store or department store.

- Instead of doing your own wedding-day shave, get pampered with some good old-fashioned grooming at your local barbershop. Call ahead to let the barber know it's a special occasion, so you won't have to wait. Take along the groom and his dad for some pre-wedding bonding.

The Basics

Of course, a good shave isn't all you need to look your wedding-day best. In the months and weeks leading up to the big day, follow these easy tips to ensure you look like a million bucks.

- Use sunscreen. There's nothing wrong with a little tan, but be sure not to get sunburned, which can lead to unsightly peeling or even blistering.

- Avoid smoking and heavy drinking, especially if you don't indulge in either very often. Overindulging can take a toll on your looks, especially if you splurge the night before the wedding. Prevent bloodshot eyes, pallid skin, and dark eye circles by drinking and smoking in moderation (or not at all).

- Exercise. Certainly a strategy you should adopt all the time, not just to lose a few pounds for your daughter's wedding. The reasons are obvious—you'll be in better health, have more energy, and look handsomer.

- Drink lots of water. The recommended daily amount is 8-ounce glasses, a half a gallon, per day. Seems like a lot, but water will give your skin a healthier appearance, it will make you feel fuller (and thus binge less). Keep a water bottle at your desk and get in the habit of sipping and refilling it numerous times during the day.

- Get enough sleep—especially the night before the wedding. You want to feel awake, vibrant, and clear-headed when you host your daughter's big day.

- Eat properly. A nice healthy balance of carbohydrates and proteins the morning of your wedding is the perfect meal. Think two hard-boiled eggs with a slice of toast; fruit and cottage cheese; a bagel with cream cheese. Nothing too fatty or heavy, unless you want to haul along a rock in your stomach as you meet and greet family and friends.

Perfect Hair

Hair is certainly not just the province of women—no matter how much or little of it you have left. For perfect wedding-day hair-do, follow these simple steps:

- Don't wait to get a haircut until the day before (or day of) the wedding. It's best to get it cut about one or two weeks in advance, so your hair has a chance to grow in a bit and lay more naturally. Ask any woman: The only cure for a bad haircut is time.

- If you're balding and uncomfortable about it, now might be the time to look into the hair replacement options you've always wondered about. Or you can continue to embrace your beautiful balding self. Just be sure to wear sunscreen at that pool party rehearsal dinner …

Hands

It doesn't matter if you work construction or perform office work, chances are the most effort you expend on your hands is the occasional obligatory fingernail clip. However, your hands are one of the most noticeable things about you. If you work in a field that leaves your fingernails permanently dirty, or you've just neglected those ragged cuticles for too long, now is the time for a professional manicure. More and more men are taking advantage of this relatively inexpensive service (usually under $20) that brings amazing results. You'll enjoy the pampering and you'll feel more comfortable shaking all those hands at the wedding and reception.

The Least You Need to Know

- Work with the bride and groom to decide upon the best style of tuxedo for you and the wedding party.

- If you work together, you and the male members of the wedding party can find bargains when it comes to renting or purchasing tuxedos and accessories.

- Personal grooming is particularly important on this, your daughter's wedding day.

- Do what it takes to feel well and well rested on the big day.

Chapter 7

Wedding Day Duties

In This Chapter

- Giving your daughter away
- What to do and say in the receiving line
- Hitting the dance floor
- A guide to tipping wedding vendors
- Going the extra mile (literally and figuratively)

Even the most laissez-faire dads will have to get involved on the wedding day, regardless of their level of past participation. So if the most you've done so far is agree to meet your daughter's fiancé, you'll have to step up to the plate on the big day. Yes, dad, it's show time, and you're a key co-star with some very important scenes.

On the other hand, if you *have* been involved in much of the wedding planning, it's finally time for all your hard work to come to fruition. Congratulate yourself privately, then bask in the shadow of your daughter's spotlight (you mustn't forget this is her day, despite all the work/time/ money you've invested).

This chapter will provide you with an overview of your wedding-day duties, many of which are steeped in tradition and some of which are simply nice-dad extras. It will give you an idea of what to expect, where these traditions came from, and how to survive each one of them. It'll also give you some hints on how to show off some of your great style along the way.

The Longest Aisle

One of dad's most visible wedding-day duties is escorting his daughter down the aisle. The tradition of the bride being "given away" by her father is as old as the hills, and some brides view it just that way: reflective of an outdated, patriarchal society with attitudes that are far from today's norm. In other words, there may be some controversy regarding this tradition, so it's best to be prepared. Your daughter may view being "given away" in a number of ways:

- A sentimental, harmless, and even beautiful tradition that honors the bond between father and daughter

- An outdated practice that offends her sensibilities, with the implication that she is mere property to be transferred to another male figure

Your daughter may have a more middle-of-the-
road view, one that doesn't balk at the tradition
but questions why mom isn't part of this whole
passing-the-torch metaphor. (Of course, in Jewish
weddings, mom has always been included, and both
parents traditionally escort the bride down the
aisle.) Even if you are the most traditional of men,
don't be surprised if the simple walk down the aisle
becomes brouhaha of dissenting opinions in your
household.

With the "giving away" tradition also comes complications that arise with stepfamilies and/or adop-
tion. Increasingly rare is the intact family unit that
includes dad who's married to mom who are both
the natural parents of the bride. If this describes
your family, great; you've got fewer touchy issues
to deal with. But there's a good chance you're read-
ing this book as your daughter's stepfather or as a
divorced dad who needs a little guidance. And if
you think *you're* confused or uncertain, the notion
of dual fathers, stepfathers, and divorced fathers
has also stymied everyone from brides to wedding
coordinators to etiquette-setters in recent years.

 Paternal Precautions _____

Make your best attempt to respect your
daughter's choices when it comes to family participation in the wedding. If you're a
stepfather or divorced dad, keep in mind
that your daughter may have some particularly difficult decisions to make.

The point is that a wedding can force to the surface long-repressed or long-buried issues. Because weddings are so public, and they force specific people to adopt specific roles, blended families can face major complications, not just logistically, but emotionally, as well …

For instance, if your daughter is very close to her stepfather (and you are her natural father), she may wish to have both of you accompany her down the aisle. On the other hand, if you have been an involved stepfather and she chooses her natural father to walk her down the aisle, your feelings may be hurt.

Whether you're a stepfather or divorced dad, keep in mind that the bride would really rather not have to make such decisions. Therefore, no matter where you stand on the issue, try to honor her wishes. The situation is not of her creation and she will simply try to make the best of a difficult, complicated family dynamic. Your daughter is not trying to hurt anyone's feelings, even if it feels that way. Rather, she is simply trying to keep the peace so she, too, can comfortably enjoy her big day. For more tips on wedding etiquette with blended families, see Chapter 9.

If you do find yourself walking your daughter down the aisle, here are a few hints to help it go smoothly:

- Walk slowly and help your daughter keep a slow, steady pace, too. If your daughter starts speeding up out of nervousness, take the lead and try to slow her down.

- Smile. Remember that there will be count-less photos documenting this little walk. If you're uncomfortable smiling, at least plaster a pleasant expression on your face.

- Look straight ahead. The most uncomfortable part of walking down the aisle is deciding where to fix your gaze, especially with all your friends and family gawking at you. For a comfortable place to focus, keep your eye on the officiant at the foot of the aisle.

- Before you take the walk down the aisle, you and your daughter will share a few minutes alone. This is a good time to say something nice, or to simply try to calm her nerves. Crack a joke or do something goofy to ease the tension.

- Carry tissues, in case the bride sheds a tear or two (or if you do, you big softie …)

- When you reach the end of the aisle, lift her veil (if she has one that covers her face) and fold it behind her head. This is when you will symbolically "give her away" to her groom. You may kiss her on the cheek or simply give her hand a squeeze— whatever you feel comfortable and natural doing.

- Some fathers also take this moment to acknowledge the groom one last time before he marries his daughter. One facetious father in New York City passed his son-in-law-to-be a flask of whiskey as he reached the end of the aisle. Presumably it was a lit-tle "medicine" for the day—or years— ahead.

- Once you are finished as her escort, take a seat at the front of the congregation.

Some Lines for the Line

There's one time in your life when it's nobler to receive than to give—and it directly follows the wedding ceremony and occurs in the receiving line. Here you'll be expected to meet and greet all the wedding guests as they exit the ceremony. You will stand alongside your daughter and new son-in-law, the bride's mother, the groom's parents, and possibly the best man and maid of honor. Additional participants may also include stepparents, if that is the bride's wish. Alternatively, you may also form a *receiving line* at the reception to welcome guests at the entrance to the party. Some brides skip the receiving line altogether, in favor of greeting guests table by table at the reception.

Dad's Definitions

The **receiving line** is a line-up formed to greet wedding guests following the ceremony (or immediately prior to the reception). The line should include the bride and groom, you, the bride's mother, the groom's parents, and possibly the maid of honor and the best man.

The tradition of the receiving line developed as a convenience, so that the families involved could greet all the guests at once, and so guests could have some personal time with the bride, groom, and their families. Some people love the receiving line for its convenience, yet others dislike it for its somewhat awkward formality and forced small talk.

The receiving line is characterized by a lot of smiling, kissing, nodding, and thanking. At its conclusion, you will feel like a skipping record, having repeated yourself countless times, over and over. It's best to be prepared for the standard receiving line dialogue so you won't be caught tongue-tied. If small talk is not your forte (and the receiving line, by its quick-moving nature, inspires some of the teeniest), then the following should help get you through it:

1. Guest: "Congratulations!"

    The diplomatic response: "Thank you, we're so happy to have Joe become part of the family." (Note: This is particularly effective among Joe's relatives.)

    The suave response: "We're happy you could share this important day with us."

    The complimentary response: "My daughter deserves all the credit. She is a wonderful young woman."

    The sarcastic response: "Congratulations? For what, going bankrupt?" (Not recommended.)

2. Guest: "So your daughter's finally leaving the nest …"

   The diplomatic response: "She's always had a good head on her shoulders."

   The suave response: "We're just happy you could share this important day with us."

   The complimentary response: "Yep, the groom is a lucky man."

   The sarcastic response: "Finally. It's time another man starts paying her credit card debt." (Not recommended.)

3. Guest: "The bride looks just beautiful …"

   The diplomatic response: "Well, she's always taken after her mother …"

   The suave response: "Yes. And we're just so happy you could share this important day with us." (As you can see, this response is terrific no matter what the guest's original comment is.)

   The sarcastic response: "Chip off the old block, heh, heh …"

Father-Daughter Dance

Your next big public role is during the father-daughter dance, which usually takes place after dinner. (Actually, your biggest task of the day is probably giving the speech, which will fall somewhere in between the ceremony and the father-daughter dance. Tips on speech-giving are covered fully in Chapter 8). The father-daughter dance is another old tradition that guests seem to love. A loving relationship between a little girl and her daddy is one of life's universal sentiments. Of course, this part of the reception may fill *you* with nothing but dread, particularly if you've spent your entire adult life avoiding the dance floor.

But whether your dance moves could be described as Fred Astaire or two left feet, the dance is a tradition your daughter will probably embrace. It may be worth a little extra effort to prepare. Anyone can master the simple box step; just ask your wife or daughter to practice with you in advance or put a little time into a pre-wedding dance class. Ask your daughter to take the class with you; not only will you learn some moves, you'll also get a chance to spend some light-hearted, quality time together before she gets married.

 "Pop"ositions

If you've never been one to glide effortlessly across the dance floor, now may be the time to learn. Check with your local YMCA or dance studio about ballroom dance classes, and ask your daughter to join you for a little father-daughter bonding before the wedding.

Of course, perfecting your dance moves is only half the battle when it comes to the father-daughter dance. The other big factor is choosing a song. There are countless tunes to choose from, and you may already share a special song with your daughter from childhood or another time. If not, here is a list of some of the more popular songs that are well-suited to sharing a twirl with your little girl.

- "A Song for My Daughter" (Ray Allaire)
- "Because You Loved Me" (Celine Dion)
- "Brown Eyed Girl" (Van Morrison)
- "Butterfly Kisses" (Bob Carlisle)
- "Can You Feel the Love Tonight" (Elton John)
- "Could Not Ask for More" (Sarah Evans)
- "Daddy's Girl" (Peter Cetera)
- "Daddy's Hands" (Holly Dunn)
- "Daddy's Little Girl" (Al Martino)
- "Don't Wanna Miss a Thing" (Aerosmith)
- "Father's Eyes" (Amy Grant)
- "Fire and Rain" (James Taylor)
- "Forever Young" (Rod Stewart or Alphaville)
- "Have I Told You Lately" (Rod Stewart)
- "Here Comes the Sun" (George Harrison)
- "Hero" (Mariah Carey)
- "How Do You Fall in Love" (Alabama)
- "I Believe in Miracles" (Engelbert Humperdink)

- "I Wish You Love" (Dean Martin)
- "If I Could" (Ray Charles)
- "In My Life" (Beatles)
- "Isn't She Lovely" (Stevie Wonder)
- "Just the Way You Are" (Billy Joel)
- "Lean on Me" (Bill Withers)
- "Little Miss Magic" (Jimmy Buffett)
- "Lullaby" (Billy Joel)
- "Memories" (Elvis Presley)
- "My Funny Valentine" (Carly Simon)
- "My Girl" (Temptations)
- "She" (Elvis Costello)
- "She's Leaving Home" (Beatles)
- "Something in the Way She Moves" (James Taylor)
- "Stand by Me" (Temptations)
- "Sunrise, Sunset" (Fiddler on the Roof soundtrack)
- "Thank Heaven for Little Girls" (Merle Haggard)
- "Thank You for Loving Me" (Bon Jovi)
- "The Dance" (Garth Brooks)
- "The Way You Do the Things You Do" (Temptations)
- "The Way You Look Tonight" (Frank Sinatra)
- "There You'll Be" (Faith Hill)
- "Time to Say Goodbye" (Sarah Brightman and Andrea Bocelli)

- "Times of Your Life" (Paul Anka)
- "Tiny Dancer" (Elton John)
- "Turn Around" (Harry Belafonte)
- "Through the Years" (Kenny Rogers)
- "Unforgettable" (Natalie Cole)
- "What a Wonderful World" (Louis Armstrong)
- "When You Love Someone" (Bryan Adams)
- "Whenever I See Your Smiling Face" (James Taylor)
- "Wind Beneath My Wings" (Bette Midler)
- "With Arms Wide Open" (Creed)
- "Wonderful Tonight" (Eric Clapton)
- "You Are So Beautiful" (Joe Cocker)
- "You Are the Sunshine of My Life" (Stevie Wonder)
- "You Belong to Me" (Patsy Cline)
- "You Decorated My Life" (Kenny Rogers)
- "You'll Be in My Heart" (Phil Collins)
- "Your Song" (Elton John)
- "You're the Inspiration" (Chicago)
- "Young at Heart" (Frank Sinatra)
- "You Make Me Feel So Young" (Frank Sinatra)

An added element you may wish to add to the father-daughter dance is a slide show, which some-one can project against a screen while you are dancing. Not only will it deflect attention from you on the dance floor, it will also provide a sentimental remembrance that all of your guests will enjoy. You may wish to start off the show with photos of you and the bride, then open it up to include your entire family, the groom, his family, and other friends and wedding guests.

Discuss in advance what will happen after your dance with the bride. Will the groom dance with his mother? Will the groom's parents share a dance? In addition to the first dance between bride and groom (which usually takes place immediately preceding the father-daughter dance), the bride and groom may wish to include other special dances: the wedding party, you and her mother (or stepmother, or current significant other), etc. Be sure to discuss these options in advance, so you are in the right place at the right time.

Tipping Guide

While not one of your "official" duties on the wedding day, you can provide some much-needed help when it comes to wedding day tipping. It'll certainly be one of the furthest things from the bride's mind, and the groom's lucky if he's even carrying his wallet that day, much less remembering to tip the service providers. You may wish to offer your help in advance, so the bride and groom know that someone will be taking care of this important task before the craziness of the day kicks in.

Father Figures

> Before tipping vendors, be sure to check on each service provider's tipping policy. Some gratuities may be included in the contractual price, and it's doubtful you'll want to tip twice, especially when you're giving a gratuity as high as 20 percent extra for the product or service pro-

You may wish to prepare tips a day or two in advance of the wedding, by setting amounts for each vendor and preparing an envelope with that amount enclosed. This strategy will prevent you from counting out loose bills from your wallet the night of the wedding, hoping you'll have enough money in the right amounts. In addition, you may wish to keep an envelope with extra cash on hand, in the event that you want to reward a vendor for extra-special service. Another rule of thumb is never tip the owner; instead tip the employees who are performing the job.

So how much are wedding vendors supposed to get? Haven't you already paid them enough? Well, no. According to etiquette, the following guidelines apply:

- Delivery staff (from the florist, bakery, etc.): 15 to 20 percent
- Officiant: $100 to $200 (or a donation to the church, the amount of which may be specifically suggested)

- Transportation: 15 to 20 percent
- Valets: $1 to $1.50 per car
- Musicians: $20 to $25 per band member
- Photographer: $20 to $25
- Wait staff: $15 to $25 per waiter, but note that a gratuity is often included in your contract so be sure to check before over-tipping
- Catering manager: $200 to $300, if not already included in your contract
- Bartender: 10 percent of liquor cost. At some weddings, a tip jar is displayed; this is a matter of taste.

Obviously, these figures are guidelines. You may decide to tip more or less based upon the service you receive and your ultimate budget. However, tips are always greatly appreciated by service providers who've worked hard to make this day a success. Though it may be tempting to skimp on tips as this bottomless pit of expenses comes to a close, be a sport and ante up.

Going the Extra Mile

There's another essential task that's perfect for dad before the wedding … map making.

Map making? For what, you may ask. Recall that many of your guests will be arriving from various areas of the country, or even the world. First they'll need to know how to get to your town and then they'll need to understand how to get around once they get there. If you live in a large city, you may want to include instructions for public transportation, subway or bus maps, or phone numbers for car services or taxis. If you live in a smaller city or suburban or rural location, driving directions may be integral to making a guest's stay comfortable and convenient. But where should you start?

First, if you'll have many out-of-town guests, suggest that your daughter send a "save the date" mailer with details regarding the wedding date and times, rehearsal dinner and times, and local accommodations. This "save the date" mailer can go out as soon as the wedding date has been set, well before the invitation is sent. Before you send it, though, you may wish to arrange a block of rooms at a hotel near all of the wedding festivities. Often hotels will provide a group rate if you guarantee a certain number of rooms. You may also wish to supply your guests with information on additional hotels, so they have a choice of suites versus rooms, or less expensive rooms at more economical hotels. Include all this information, including hotel names, phone numbers, and information on group discounts in the *save the date* mailer. You should also include information on the nearest airport(s) and, again, provide guests with an option if one exists.

Dad's Definitions

A **save the date** mailer alerts guests of the impending wedding date, and it is usually sent out months before the big day. It's particularly useful if you're inviting many out-of-town guests, as it gives them ample time to make travel arrangements.

Within the wedding invitations, which will be sent out approximately six to eight weeks before the wedding, you may wish to provide more detailed directions to and from important weekend locations. For instance, include maps or detailed driving directions from the airport to the hotel you've recommended, and then from the hotel to the ceremony and/or reception site. It's extremely important to provide directions or even group transportation to and from main venues. For example, if the majority of your out-of-town guests will be staying at one hotel, you might want to hire a shuttle to bring them to the wedding and back. This strategy will also help prevent guests from drinking and driving, which is always an important concern.

So how should you get these directions? There are a number of ways to go about it if you don't already know the route. The first is to call the hotel or reception site and ask for directions from key locations such as the airport or the train station. You can also get directions to and from virtually anywhere online. One great site is www.mapquest.com. Enter your starting location and destination and you'll be provided with detailed driving directions and a map you can print out, free of charge. Once you get directions from either of these sources, you may wish to do a trial run to make sure they are clear and accurate.

 "Pop"ositions

It's a great courtesy to your guests to provide directions to and from each wedding destination (the ceremony site, reception site, rehearsal dinner location, etc.) Be sure to provide accurate, detailed directions and addresses so they'll be sure to arrive intact and on time.

If most of your guests won't be driving at all (if the wedding is in NYC or another large city, for example) provide detailed subway maps or bus maps and don't assume everyone will take cabs. Highlight routes from place to place, so getting there's a no-brainer even for those country relatives who've never ventured into the big city before.

Another courtesy you can provide to your out-of-town guests is information about the local area, particularly if there is any downtime during which they're not expected to be at wedding-related events. If they are staying in a hotel, provide "welcome baskets" with bottled water, snacks, and information on local attractions, restaurants, and/or

special events. You may also wish to include a letter
to welcome them and give them a run-down of the
weekend's itinerary.

The Least You Need to Know

- If you're part of a divorced or blended family, your daughter may have some difficult decisions to make; try to respect her choices.

- There are countless wedding songs to choose from, in genres ranging from rock to pop to country to easy listening (and much more).

- Tipping vendors is the ideal task for dad to take on during the hubbub of the wedding day; prepare ahead of time to simplify this job.

- Preparing your guests with detailed information on travel, accommodations, and transportation is another way to help ensure the wedding goes smoothly.

Father Knows Best

In This Chapter

- A speech that will keep your guests riveted
- Hosting with panache
- Wedding gift ideas

When it comes to certain topics, we all know that *Father Knows Best*. And even when he doesn't, sometimes he'd better look as if he does. Case in point: your daughter's wedding day. Not only do you want to look your best, you also want to behave at your best. That doesn't mean simply avoiding keg stands and beer chugging, as in your younger days. Instead, it means bringing out all the charm, style, and panache you've accumulated through your vast and varied worldly experiences.

This chapter will provide some tips that will help you unleash your inner charm, whether you're giving a wedding day speech, greeting guests, or choosing a perfect gift for the bride and groom.

A Toast with the Most

You may be an old pro at public speaking, with countless work-related speeches and presentations under your standard-issue, corporate-logo belt buckle. In fact, you may enjoy public speaking tremendously. After all, how often do you find all the attention riveted on you? At the risk of answering a question with a question, why do you think bands like the Rolling Stones and Aerosmith keep touring, despite the fact that they need neither the money nor the notoriety? They're addicted to the rush of adoration, to the excitement of being the center of attention.

You, dad, can be the Mick Jagger of your daughter's wedding. Of course, it's more likely you count yourself among the 99 percent of Americans who dread the public light. In fact, so many dislike of public speaking that it is documented as America's #1 greatest fear. It's a bigger fear than going to the dentist. Bigger, even, than death.

However, it doesn't have to be that way. If you've ever given speeches, you know that the more you give them, the more comfortable it becomes. With some simple preparation and few strategies, you, too, can be comfortable with public speaking and impress your guests at the same time. (Throw in a few of Mick's dance moves, and there's no telling what can happen …

Writing the Speech

Before you can deliver a speech, of course, you need to write it. But if writing anything more than a grocery list gives you goose bumps, writing the speech is easier said than done. Use the following tips to help ease the stress—and writer's block—you may be experiencing.

- **Start soon**. It's never too early to begin thinking about your speech. The more preparation time you give yourself, the more time you'll have for your ideas to "marinate." In other words, you may think something that's funny today is just silly tomorrow, but only time will tell. Keep the ideas that play as well in April as they did in January, and toss the rest of 'em.

"Pop"ositions

Your speech does not have to be brilliantly written or perfectly delivered to be a success. Most likely you will be the only person to notice any mistakes.

- **Write down your ideas.** You're driving to work, and you suddenly recall a humorous moment you shared with your daughter. Quick! Jot it down! Or risk forgetting it a day later, when 50 more interfering thoughts have erased it from your consciousness.

- **Simplify your story**. If you follow a simple structure like: "This is where I was. This is where I am. And this is how I got here," it's easy to fill in the blanks. For instance, perhaps 10 years ago you were watching your daughter with a new boyfriend every week. And now you are witnessing her settling down with just one. Telling the story of how A. led to B. will provide an interesting, complete, and (hopefully) humorous story.

- **Remember your audience**. Everyone is there to celebrate. Obviously, your speech should remain positive and enthusiastic. Some occasional light-hearted ribbing is okay, but you should never discuss sensitive topics that might hurt feelings. That means you'll include nothing critical of the groom, and nothing critical of the bride. Not that you would.

- **Start with a catchy opening.** Put your audience at ease immediately. Some experts recommend starting with a joke or funny anecdote, but anything that engages your audience's attention is fair game. Your opening should also allude to, and segue way nicely, into the body of the speech. In other words, don't tell a joke that has absolutely no connection to what you're about to say.

- **Limit your speech to three or four main points**. Try not to go off on too many tangents. For instance, if your idea is to tell some funny anecdotes about your daughter and/or the groom, limit it to three or four short stories, and make sure they relate to one another. For example, you may start out with a story about how your daughter resisted piano lessons her whole childhood. Which leads to how she grew up and decided to take up piano again in college. Which leads to the fact that she meets the groom in her college piano class. Which leads to the punch line—if it weren't for dad pushing those darn piano lessons, she wouldn't be getting married today.

Paternal Precautions

Don't try to cover too many points in your speech, and don't try to please everyone. Your audience is varied, but if you remember they all have one thing in common—their good wishes for the bride and groom—you'll craft a perfectly toned message.

- **Create an outline.** It's always much easier if you jot down the main ideas of your speech before actually sitting down to write it. Let the writing flow from there.

- **End the speech on an up-note**. Finish with a punch line, an inspirational story, or some heartfelt words to the bride and groom. Thank the audience for their attention. Then get ready to bask in the glow of the compliments you're bound to receive.

Delivering Your Speech

Now that you've written the perfect speech, you really wish someone *else* could deliver it. Never fear: Following a few simple suggestions, you'll be ready to deliver your speech like the best of politicians.

- **Maintain eye contact.** Obviously, establishing eye contact with 300 guests is impossible. Encourage your guests to become more involved in your speech. Choose a few key tables nearby and focus on them throughout your speech. Keep an eye on the friendly, laughing faces to boost your confidence once you get started. Remember, this is an audience that fully supports you. They want you to succeed.

- **Use notes if necessary.** Obviously, if your eyes stay glued to your notes the entire time, you'll contradict the previous point, which is to maintain eye contact. Do your best to memorize your speech beforehand to avoid this problem, but feel free to keep your notes on hand if your memory suddenly fails you. Practice your speech often before the wedding day. You'll be amazed at how much it's seeped into your subconscious when it comes time to deliver it.

"Pop"ositions

The most important thing to remember when delivering your speech is to *just be yourself*. Don't try to emulate another's speaking style, or sense of humor, or body language. Ultimately you'll give the best speech if do what comes naturally.

- **Mind your body language**. Don't sway, tap your foot, tap your fingers, or move any other body part besides your mouth (unless, of course, you always talk with your hands, in which case it's more important to act naturally). A comfortable position for your arms is simply relaxed by your sides.

- **Be aware of your facial expression**. A pleasant look or smile is always appropriate.

- **Project your voice.** If you're hosting a large reception for a few hundred guests, you may wish to arrange use of a microphone. In fact, all but the most voluminous speakers won't be heard in a large venue. Put energy into delivering your speech, infusing it with pitch to convey emotion, and differentiating your volume to emphasize the most important points. Avoid sounding monotone or emotionless. If you can, practice with the microphone so you're comfortable with it come toast-time.

- **Involve your audience.** One of the best ways to break the tension of public speaking is to involve audience members by creating a give-and-take with them. Ask them questions, engage their sense of humor (laughter always eases the tension of a silent room), or solicit their feedback.

- **Control the butterflies.** Even the most practiced public speakers and performers still get jittery preceding a performance—it's perfectly natural. The best way to combat the physical symptoms of nervousness (sweaty palms, rapid heartbeat, shallow breathing) is to do some deep breathing exercises immediately before your speech. Take slow, deep breaths to calm yourself. If your symptoms are severe, which certainly would keep you from feeling comfortable delivering your speech, you may also wish to talk to your doctor about medicine that can control it. Prescription beta blockers are often prescribed to ease physical manifestations of stress. They regulate the heartbeat so it won't race and trigger all those other symptoms. Obviously, you should check with your doctor before taking any prescription drugs.

- **Don't drown your fears.** You haven't come this far, dad, without knowing that too much of a good thing is usually a bad thing. While a cocktail or two before your speech may calm your nerves, any more than that will put you at risk of forgetting your speech, slurring your words, or otherwise compromising your ability to speak like a respectable adult.

- **Don't be too hard on yourself.** When all is said and done, don't berate yourself afterward for forgetting a particular sentence or stumbling over a word. Your guests probably didn't even notice—or if they did, they're certainly not focusing on it. Instead, your guests will come away thinking about the anecdotes or main message in your speech.

"Pop"ositions

Another good speech strategy is to speak humbly, and reveal something about you. Few people respond well to false bravado or a display of over-inflated ego.

Hosting with Panache

In this and the previous chapter, you've received tips designed to help you perform all of your specific duties, including escorting your daughter down the aisle, the father-daughter dance, your speech, and more. But what are you supposed to do in between these activities? How are you supposed to act? Well, assuming you're the wedding's host (an honor that becomes yours by assuming the bills), it's your job to take on a host's responsibility. But what, exactly, does this mean?

Simply put, a good host is hyper-aware of his guests' feelings. As you've probably picked up over the years, it's a lot more fun to be a guest than a host. As host you're responsible not just for your own good time but for all your guests' good times as well.

You are also responsible for ensuring that all the elements of the party flow smoothly. In the case of your daughter's wedding, being a good host means keeping an eye on all the important matters, including the passing of hors d'oeuvres, the bar, guest seating, dinner service, music, the cake, and much more.

In addition, there are some miscellaneous duties you should try to fulfill:

- If a guest is standing alone or appears uncomfortable, take him or her under your wing. Introduce him or her to another guest or help him or her join another group's chatter. You may also help direct this guest to his or her table to meet the other guests who are sitting there.

- Keep an eye on the bar. If it's suddenly three-deep with waiting guests, talk to the catering manager to determine if there's someone else available to pitch in to bartend. Often wedding bars experience rush times, including when guests first arrive and immediately before dinner, especially if you're temporarily closing the bar in favor of dinnertime wine service.

- Keep an eye, on the hors d'oeuvres distribution. If the party features butler-passed vittles, make sure the waiters are circulating among the guests, not just concentrating on those closest to the kitchen. If guests have ravenously cleared your crudités display halfway through the cocktail hour, ask if the kitchen can supply more (if the budget allows, of course).

- Monitor your musicians. If they are scheduled to play after dinner, for instance, you may wish to take on the responsibility of giving them their "cue" to begin during dessert.

- Watch for wayward guests. Inevitably there will be one or two ladies or gentlemen who end up imbibing a bit too much during the festivities. And while weddings are occasions to celebrate, the fun ends when one of these guests plans to get behind the wheel. Provide alternate transportation, whether it's a cab or a lift home with a sober guest.

- Talk to your guests. Your role as "enforcer" (see above) shouldn't eclipse your role as host. Take the time to enjoy as many guests as possible, from both your side and the groom's side.

- Take a twirl. Take the time to dance to at least a few songs. If there are women guests attending alone, it's also chivalrous to ask them to dance—especially recently widowed or divorced guests who may be uncomfortable being alone.

- Share a private toast with the groom's parents. Presumably you've all been through a lot during these months of planning, so take a moment to bond (especially if there have been any strained relations).

- Acknowledge the wedding party. Most likely they've put in great deal of effort to be part of this wedding, including financial commitments (clothing, travel, hosting showers, and bachelor or bachelorette parties) and time commitments.

- Take some time just for you. Sweep your wife off her feet on the dance floor; share a cigar or after-dinner aperitif with a close friend or relative. After all, you, too, should enjoy the spoils of your efforts.

The Perfect Wedding Gift

In your family, simply throwing your daughter's wedding may be gift enough. And if you're throwing the "average" wedding, that "gift" may cost you from $15,000 to $20,000, which is a very generous offering by anyone's standards.

However, many families wish to give an additional wedding gift that the wedding couple can keep and cherish for a lifetime. If the bride and groom have thrown the wedding themselves, you may be in a position to give them a more substantial gift. But what could you possibly give to your daughter, after all the cookware and linens and vacuum cleaners and kitchen appliances you've seen darkening your doorstep over the past few months? Hasn't she already received everything a person could possibly need at the showers, engagement parties, and the wedding itself?

Well, yes and no. As her father, you'll probably want to give her something a little more personal than a food processor or a set of monogrammed towels, something that will have lasting value. It may be something that she can pass on to her own children.

 Father Figures _____

> You don't have to purchase an expensive wedding gift to make an impact. In fact, more thoughtful gifts are usually more meaningful. It can be as simple as a scrapbook you prepare with pictures and mementos or the passing-on of a family heirloom that she's always admired.

Buying gifts can be a difficult endeavor and you may or may not have a lot of experience with it. If the extent of your gift shopping is your once-a-year trip to the jewelers for your wife at Christmas, it's time to read ahead for some creative wedding gift ideas.

The following offer some ideas to get you started.

- An original piece of artwork by a favorite artist

- A framed photograph or watercolor of the ceremony or reception site

- A beautiful bowl or vase of crystal, hand-made pottery, metal, or ceramics (whatever their taste)

- A first edition signed antique book by their favorite author(s)

- A leather-bound bible

- Furniture for their home, such as a dining room or living room set, or a special piece you've shopped for, such as an antique table or lamp (be sure it's to their taste, not yours)

- A honeymoon (pay for transportation and accommodations)

- A car (for those with bucks to burn)

- Down payment on a house (for those with even more bucks to burn)

- An airplane voucher (so that they can come visit you if they live faraway)

- Tickets for your whole family to a future event (football game, art exhibit, philharmonic concert, whatever you'd all enjoy together)

- A gift certificate to your city's finest, most expensive restaurant (something they'd never buy themselves)

- An interesting gift that would be impractical for them to buy themselves, such as a hand-carved chess set, a standing globe, or an extravagant gadget from a specialty store like The Sharper Image
- Outdoor furniture, a grill, or a pool
- Contractor costs (or a certificate to Home Depot), to remodel or update a home
- Landscaping services
- A hand-painted mailbox or "Welcome" sign for their home
- A membership to a wine-of-the-month, beer-of-the-month, or food-of-the-month club (fruit, steaks, even potato chips are options)
- Sports or hobby-related gifts, such as membership to a ski, tennis, or golf club; a seasonal lift ticket for the bride and groom; new tennis racquets, skis or golf clubs (especially if you all play together); a treadmill or universal gym; his and hers mountain bikes; etc.
- Cash, to use whatever way they'd like (wedding expenses, housing costs, honeymoon expenses, etc.)

The Least You Need to Know

- With some time, practice, and a few key strategies, you can write and deliver a wedding-day toast that's meaningful and memorable.

- Monitoring your guests' ongoing comfort and good time is the essential duty of a quality host.

- The perfect wedding gift is usually the result of a little creativity and legwork, not necessarily a high price tag.

Chapter 9

Sticky Situations

In This Chapter

- Handling the groom's family
- Dealing with stepfamily issues
- Handling racial, religious, or ethnic differences
- Troubleshooting unexpected situations

No matter how organized you are, how well you plan, or how exquisite your taste, there's simply no way you'll produce a perfectly smooth wedding from beginning to end. The problem is that human emotion—and error—always gets in the way. And the greater number of humans involved (i.e., stepparents, siblings, and your future "in-laws"), the less smooth it's bound to be. Then there are your vendors, most of whom will try their hardest to do a great job, but some of who will, inevitably, disappoint you. (If only this process were automated ...)

Unfortunately, the only thing you can control is your own behavior. And while it may seem like a spit in the punch bowl, it's often enough to set an example so that others can follow suit. This chapter provides some examples of sticky situations you may encounter, and some strategies to make the best of them in order to preserve family harmony as you count down the days to the big event.

The Q&A format is intended to answer commonly-asked questions when it comes to handling uncomfortable wedding-related situations, ranging from in-law trouble to stepfamily stress.

Welcome to the Family

There's no doubt that many a wedding is almost derailed due to differences of opinion among "the families." While the bride and groom may agree on everything, their mothers may not. And if these mothers are the doting, overbearing type, it can lead to real conflict.

You, dad, have the opportunity to act as the voice of reason and the ambassador of diplomacy with the groom's family. Embrace this challenge with all the charm and goodwill we know you have. For some extra support, the following provides some tips on handling specific situations you may encounter.

The Odd Couple

Q: We really like our daughter's fiancé, but his parents are another story. We simply have nothing in common with them. How should we handle this situation?

A: This is a common problem, if only because you and the groom's parents have been thrown into a situation in which you're forced to get along and socialize even though you are virtual strangers to one another. Though it appears as if you have nothing in common (they're millionaires and you're middle class, they're liberals and you're conservatives, they're loud and boisterous and you're quiet and mild-mannered) there's one important thing that you do have in common: your daughter and their son. So when all else fails, talk about the bride and groom.

 "Pop"ositions

If you're lucky, you may find yourselves getting along famously with the groom's parents. Feel free to extend your friendship beyond wedding events, such as sharing the occasional evening out or holiday.

But what, exactly, are you physically required to do with these people during the months leading up to the wedding? First, you're required to meet them, and formal etiquette dictates that they should be the ones to issue an invitation. If an invite has not been forthcoming, however, you may wish to issue one yourself.

After your initial meeting, you'll probably also be in contact with them to take care of necessary wedding business, such as sharing guest lists, discussing finances, or arranging for pre-wedding parties such as showers, engagement parties, or the rehearsal dinner. It is polite to confer with the other family before formally setting a date for any party.

You are not required to become best friends with them, but you should always be cordial. This is for your daughter's sake as much as your own. No matter how distasteful it may seem to you, you'll be seeing these people at your family's big events for years to come. Make this and future occasions as pleasant as possible.

Hey, Big Spender

Q: My daughter's fiancé's parents have offered to split the cost of the wedding. We'd rather pay for it ourselves. What should we do?

A: Formal etiquette dictates that it is perfectly acceptable for the bride's family to turn down any offer of financial assistance from the groom's family. You may choose to do so for a number of reasons: You wish to retain control over the planning process; you sense that any donation would entitle them to become overbearing and opinionated, a situation you'd rather avoid; you feel that paying for your daughter's wedding is simply your responsibility. It doesn't matter what your reasons are; you are still entitled to reject their offer.

When doing so, be sure to act with diplomacy. Regardless of etiquette, they may feel insulted that you're rejecting their generosity. No matter what your reasons, try to couch them with something nonthreatening. Tell them you've had a wedding fund earmarked for this occasion for years, and you feel it is your responsibility to cover the whole cost. If they're truly generous, and it's not simply an attempt to share control of the wedding planning, they'll give the bride and groom the money for something else such as the honeymoon, or toward a home.

Of course, you may also wish to consider accepting their generous offer. Don't let pride get in the way of practical financial decision-making, particularly if your daughter's dream wedding is going to really strain your finances. Though their offer may come with some strings attached, in the end it may be easier to compromise than to risk financial ruin.

Show Me the Money

Q: We've met a number of times with the groom's family, and we get along well with them. However, they haven't once made any offer to contribute financially to the wedding. Our other son-in-law's parents paid for the bar and some other wedding expenses, and we expected a similar offer from this family. Should we say something?

A: There's nothing like the uncomfortable talk of money to start a new relationship. Formal etiquette dictates that the bride's family pay the lion's share of the wedding expenses, excluding the rehearsal dinner, the bridal bouquet, and certain other expenses (see Chapter 4 for the breakdown). Unfortunately, some people aren't aware of the formal etiquette, or just don't have the resources to cover these expenses.

In any case, it's not advisable that you bring the topic up with them, no matter how friendly you all are (unless you want those good relations to fade quickly). If you really need to, try to learn through the "grapevine" whether they are planning to contribute (i.e., the groom talks to his parents, the groom tells the bride, the bride tells you). No matter what you find out, try not to make a federal case of it; perhaps they're undergoing financial difficulties right now, or they simply don't have the money. They may be embarrassed to admit this, and that's why they haven't brought up the topic.

If you suspect they're just being cheap, suck it up. There's nothing you can do to change or control their behavior, and attempting to do so will just frustrate you. Let it go, so that you can enjoy the planning and excitement leading up to the wedding without hard feelings.

What's the Word?

Q: How should we word the invitations if we're sharing expenses with the groom's family?

A: See Appendix A for invitation wording for every contingency.

Step-ping Out

Stepfamilies and divorce seem to be the root of a great deal of the stress associated with wedding planning. Because they are so public in nature, weddings force all the issues to be dealt with at once, including such touchy issues as where should everyone sit, who should give the first toast, who should dance with the bride, how invitations should be worded, etc. The bride typically bears the brunt of this stress, as she is ultimately responsible for many of these decisions. You can help, too, by being aware of the dynamics and responding to her decisions maturely.

Second Class Citizen

Q: I love my daughter like she's my own, even though she is my stepdaughter. But I'm feeling that she's leaving me out of many of the wedding traditions in favor of her "real" father (who I feel hasn't really been there over the years). How should I deal with this?

A: Your stepdaughter is probably just as uncomfortable with the situation as you are, and unless she's a nasty, vindictive person, she'd rather not have to choose alliances. If you two are close, you may wish to express your hurt feelings to her, but try not to lay on a guilt trip. She's probably already given this a lot of thought and feels she's made the best decision for her, whether it's choosing her "real" father to give her away, to dance with her at the reception, or to deliver the toast.

You may also wish to express your feelings to your wife, who may be able to talk to your daughter more gently about the situation. Or she may be able to explain to you why your daughter has made the decisions she has. In any case, try to support the bride's ultimate decisions and be a good sport; your daughter will love you more for it in the end.

The Real Deal

Q: My daughter wants to give equal billing to her stepfather at the wedding. I don't think this is fair; after all, I'm her natural father. What should I do?

A: Do you think it's fair that your daughter has to make this decision in the first place? Point: Life isn't fair or easy, as you no doubt already know.

Your best bet in this situation is to respect your daughter's wishes. Presumably she has a close relationship with her stepfather—perhaps he helped raise her, and she wants to acknowledge that fact. Instead of embracing your natural reaction—jealousy—try to look at it another way. Your daughter is lucky to have grown up close to both you and her stepfather; this is a much better outcome, in the end, than if she had a terrible relationship with him.

There's no better way to handle the situation than in a dignified manner. While you're sharing the spotlight with stepdad, all your guests will no doubt notice how much grace under pressure you exhibit.

Calling a Truce

Q: I can't stand to be in the same room as my daughter's mother (we're divorced), and I'm dreading this whole wedding because of it. Help!

A: If you think you're worried about this situation, you should get into your daughter's head for a few minutes. Her dream of a perfect day with no glitches, embarrassment, or complications is being put at serious risk by two adults who she knows just can't get along.

"Pop"ositions

You loved her mother enough once to create a child; try to tap into something that doesn't resemble hostility during the engagement and wedding, if only to benefit your daughter. It may be a challenge, but we know you can do it.

The greatest wedding gift you can give your daughter is to turn the other cheek. Again, the only behavior you can control is your own. Even if the root cause of the problem is ultimately your ex-wife (and everybody knows it), all you can do is control your own reaction to her. And for your daughter's sake, the best reaction is no reaction, even if it takes forcing every cell, atom, and electron in your body to behave.

No matter what the reasons for your divorce with the bride's mother, try to set any resentment or bad feelings aside, at least during the few occasions you find yourself thrown together. You'll be a bigger man for it, and no doubt everyone else will notice it, too.

Unconventional Weddings

No matter what, weddings are a challenge to plan. Between all the details that need settling and all the opinions that need weighing, it's amazing that any wedding actually takes place. Throw in a complication, like an extra religion, an unfamiliar ethnicity, or an unplanned pregnancy, and things can get really hairy.

Keeping the Faith

Q: My daughter is marrying a man of another faith. While we weren't enthusiastic initially, we have come to support their decision to marry. Any tips for the wedding day and beyond?

A: As America continues to be a melting pot and people are increasingly exposed to more diversity through travel and education, "unconventional" unions are becoming more and more the norm. And whether it's a difference of race, religion, politics, ethnicity, or geography, the news may be a bit hard to swallow initially. Presumably, however, you've raised your daughter to make intelligent decisions. While a cross-race or cross-religion marriage may pose unique challenges, it will also pose unique opportunities to learn and grow.

Paternal Precautions

When it comes to interracial or cross-religion (or even cross-regional) marriages, the key is compromise. Include traditions of both the bride and groom at the ceremony and the reception, and understand that the couple may begin their own traditions beyond the wedding day.

During the wedding itself, your daughter may consider including elements from both cultures to symbolize the marriage as a whole. For instance, if it's a Jewish/Christian wedding, you may wish to include both a rabbi and a minister to perform the wedding ceremony, or to hold two separate wedding ceremonies with each religion's traditions kept wholly intact. This way, both families will feel as if their faith and traditions are represented.

Of course, the wedding is only one day and you're more concerned, frankly, about the rest of their lives. What sorts of traditions will they honor? What religion will they adopt for their children? And where do you fit into all of this? Obviously, these are questions for your daughter and her husband to work out. The best strategy for you to take is to listen before you speak, and to keep an open mind. Remember, your daughter's choice of husband is not a slight at you, but simply the result of who she fell in love with. Unless you wish to alienate your daughter, it's a fact you'll eventually need to deal with.

Bun In the Oven

Q: My daughter will be pregnant when she marries. How, as her dad, am I supposed to deal with this?

A: As a father, there's no doubt that you have mixed emotions about your daughter's marriage particularly if it's been accelerated due to pregnancy. However, remaining calm and understanding is never a bad approach when dealing with a stressful situation. Anger or disappointment with either the bride or the groom, while it may be natural, won't solve the problem. You should simply try to make the best of a complicated situation. After all, they are getting married, which is a responsible first step in creating a stable home for the new child and reason enough to celebrate.

Depending upon how many months along your daughter's pregnancy is, you may or may not wish to make this fact public. Obviously, if she's six months pregnant, there's not much hope of hiding it. However, if she's just three months along there may be little outward evidence of the fact. This is a judgement call that only you and your family can make.

As for the nature of the wedding celebration, you can set any tone you like. It can be a traditional celebration with hundreds of guests, or a more intimate affair including close family and friends. Do whatever you feel comfortable with, but remember this is meant to be a pleasant, happy occasion, so treat it justly.

Acts of God (or God-Like Vendors)

Among the most organized of families, there's only so much you can control (unless you're a Soprano, that is). The following situations may arise, no matter how well you plan. Fortunately, we offer you some simple solutions that may just save the day.

Possessed by Pew Bows

Q: Help! My daughter has turned into Bridezilla! A high-maintenance, greedy monster has replaced her practical, sensible side. What should I do?

A: Unfortunately, dad, this large-scale possession can happen to even the most level-head woman once she gets that ring on her finger. Luckily, the demon is usually miraculously exorcised on the plane trip home from the honeymoon. But how to handle it until then?

It's tough to fight the beast. Many women have bought into the notion that this is the most important day of their lives, and as such has to be absolutely, 100 percent perfect. Unfortunately, her idea of perfect can run you $20,000 or much, much more if you let it. And while this day is important, it's only a party, a symbol of what's really important, which is the decision to spend the rest of her life with someone.

If she's Bridezilla, she obviously doesn't share this sentiment at the moment. For now, all she's thinking about is that wedding day. And aside from repeatedly putting things into perspective for her, there's little you can do apart from controlling the purse strings. As much as you may want to give her everything her heart desires, this simply isn't practical, unless you're a multimillionaire (and even then, is $7000 on flowers that will die in 24 hours really rational?) Don't feel guilty calming the beast, especially when she starts getting grandiose notions of taking over the entire city.

Let the Music Play ...

Q: It's a week before the wedding, and the band cancelled. My daughter is hyperventilating in her room. What can I do?

A: First of all, understand that this seems like the end of the world to your daughter, who has eaten, breathed, and dreamed nothing but this wedding for the last six or nine or twelve months (in other words, she's lost some perspective on life). On the other hand, a party without music is a bit of a bummer. What you can do, however, is save the day.

Start calling everyone you know for names of bands, DJs, their kids' garage ensemble, whatever. Anything of decent quality will do at this point, and your daughter may have to be flexible with her choice. Although she wanted a Latin jazz band, she may have to settle for a six-piece swing band. If all else fails and there are simply no professional bands or DJs available, look into renting equipment and spinning your own music. Employ the help of family and friends to burn some special CDs; make it a team effort. Then ask if a young relative would mind being DJ for the night, and make it worth his or her while with a few bucks.

Use similar tactics if other vendors, such as the photographer or baker, should bail out at the last minute.

But Can I Keep the Ring?

Q: My daughter has called off her engagement three weeks before the wedding date. What do we do?

A: Before you do anything, allow a day or two to pass just in case it's simply a case of pre-wedding jitters instead of a permanent break. Once you know the wedding definitely is off, you'll need to act fast. If you've already mailed the invitations, etiquette dictates that you should send a formal printed card announcing the cancellation. However, if there is simply not enough time to have cards printed and mailed, a personal note or phone call is also appropriate. In a real emergency, e-mail will suffice, but avoid it if possible because it's too informal for the occasion.

Call out-of-towners first, so they can cancel their travel plans if they wish. Calls can be made by you, the bride's mother, or by anyone on your behalf.

You'll also need to look at your vendor contracts as soon as possible for cancellation policies. There's no doubt you'll lose all your down payments, but you may also be liable for additional expenses depending on the timing. Cancellation with short notice prevents a caterer, band, or photographer from getting another gig for the same date, so they may penalize you.

Then, of course, there are the emotional issues to deal with. Your daughter needs her dad more now than ever, so try to provide a shoulder to lean on. No doubt she is devastated right now, no matter what the reason is for the cancellation. Be her rock.

The Least You Need to Know

- Diplomacy is key when dealing with the groom's family—whether you're discussing wedding finances, wedding plans, or the weather.

- Be sensitive to your daughter's tough choices when it comes to appeasing step-parents and natural parents. It's not easy pleasing everyone.

- Even if you feel the bride and groom may not be perfectly compatible, keep an open mind and a cool head or risk alienating your daughter. You may end up surprised at what a great match they really are.

- When unexpected challenges arise, it's your opportunity to lend a hand and save the day.

Appendix A

Wedding Words

boutonniere   A single bloom or bud attached to the left lapel of a man's jacket. The father of the bride, the groom, the attendants, ushers, and the groom's father typically wear these.

destination wedding   A celebration at a chosen location away from home (European and tropical locations are popular), at which the bride and groom marry surrounded by a small group of family members and friends.

personal shower   A girls-only party that's usually smaller and more exclusive than the "typical" shower. The bride may receive more personal gifts such as lingerie, and the party is usually thrown by close girlfriends, sisters, or other close female relatives.

receiving line   A line-up formed to greet wedding guests following the ceremony (or immediately prior to the reception). The line should include the bride and groom, you, the bride's mother, the groom's parents, and possibly the maid of honor and the best man.

save the date mailer   A "pre-invitation" that alerts guests of the impending wedding date, which is usually sent out months before the big day. It's particularly useful if you're inviting many out-of-town guests, as it gives them ample time to make travel arrangements.

theme wedding   Any wedding that incorporates an overriding concept or creative idea. Examples of theme weddings include medieval weddings, 1920's weddings, underwater weddings, Victorian weddings, or holiday weddings such as Valentine's Day, Halloween, or Christmas soirees.

wedding favor   Small gifts given to wedding guests. Common favors include candies or chocolates, small picture frames (which double as place cards), and flower or plant seeds or blossoms. Favors also provide a great way to individualize a wedding celebration, with unusual or personalized items.

weekend wedding   A celebration consisting of weekend-long events beyond simply the wedding and reception, which may include meals, sporting events, or other get-togethers in the days preceding and following the wedding day.

Wording Wedding Invitations

How an invitation is worded says a lot about the event being thrown—including who is hosting or sponsoring it (but not necessarily who's paying for it …) Typically, the bride's family issues the invitation, and there is standard wording that reflects this situation. But what if your family has more complicated circumstances, like divorced parents, stepparents, or widowed parents? What if you want to include the groom's family? Or what if you wish only to include the bride's and groom's names—with no one "sponsoring" the wedding at all? This section provides wording for these seemingly complex situations and more.

When the Bride's Family Acts as Hosts

This is the most frequently used wording that reflects the traditional, bridal-sponsored wedding:

Mr. and Mrs. Michael Smith
request the honor of your presence
at the marriage of their daughter

Gabrielle Jane

to

Jonathan Brown

Saturday, the tenth of June
at five o'clock
Holy Angels Church
Buffalo, New York

When the Bride's and Groom's Family Share Hosting Duties

If you'd like to include the groom's parents, as well, but they are not co-hosting or "co-sponsoring" the wedding, formal etiquette suggests the following:

Mr. and Mrs. Michael Smith
request the honor of your presence
at the marriage of their daughter

Gabrielle Jane

to

Jonathan Brown

son of Mr. and Mrs. William Brown
Saturday, the tenth of June …

When the bride's and groom's families both "sponsor" or host the wedding, you may try the following wording. Note that this wording does not clearly spell out the relationship of the parents to each individual child (i.e., there may be some confusion among more distant relatives or friends).

Mr. and Mrs. Michael Smith
and Mr. and Mrs. William Brown
request the pleasure of your company
at the marriage of their children

Gabrielle Jane

and

Jonathan Edward

Saturday, the tenth of June
at five o'clock
Holy Angels Church
Buffalo, New York

Invitations from Divorced Parents

In general, when the bride's parents are divorced, the invitation is issued by the parent who raised her. The following options cover various contingencies.

When Mom Has Not Remarried

If the bride's divorced mother is issuing the invitation, and she is not remarried, she may word her name in a number of ways. She may use both her maiden name and married surname, preceded by "Mrs." (Mrs. McCoy Martin), or she may opt for her first name, maiden name and married surname (Susan McCoy Martin).

> Susan McCoy Martin
> requests the honor of your presence
> at the marriage of her daughter
>
> Gabrielle Jane …

When an Un-remarried Dad Issues the Invitation

If the invitation will be issued by you, her father, and you have not remarried, it should be worded as follows:

> Mr. Michael Smith
> requests the honor of your presence
> at the marriage of his daughter
>
> Gabrielle Jane …

If you are remarried, you may adopt the following:

> Mr. and Mrs. Michael Smith
> request the honor of your presence
> at the marriage of Mr. Smith's daughter
>
> Gabrielle Jane …

Note: If the bride is close to her stepmother, you may wish to substitute "their daughter" for "Mr. Smith's daughter."

When Divorced Parents Issue Invitation Together

If you and the bride's mother are still friendly, you may wish to send the invitation together. So as not to confuse guests, list your names on separate lines:

Susan McCoy Martin
(or Mrs. John Andrews, if remarried)
and
James Edward Martin
(or Mr. James Edward Martin)
request the honor of your presence
at the marriage of their daughter

Gabrielle Jane ...

When the Groom's Parents Are Divorced

If you plan to also include the groom's parents on the invitation, and the groom's parents are divorced, use the following as a guideline:

Mr. and Mrs. James Martin
request the honor of your presence
at the marriage of their daughter

Gabrielle Jane

to

Jonathan Edward

son of
Mrs. Florence Ives
and
Mr. William Brown

When Dad Is Widowed

If you are a widower who has not remarried, the following wording may be appropriate:

> Mr. James Martin
> requests the honor of your presence
> at the marriage of his daughter
>
> Gabrielle Jane ...

If you are widowed and remarried, try the following:

> Mr. and Mrs. James Martin
> request the honor of your presence
> at the marriage of Mr. Martin's daughter
>
> Gabrielle Jane ...

If the bride is close to her stepmother, you may also use "their daughter" in place of "Mr. Martin's daughter."

Under Other Circumstances

You may also find yourself hosting the wedding with someone else, such as a live-in partner, the bride's grandmother, or aunt, etc. In this case, you may wish to adopt the following wording:

> Mr. James Martin
> and
> Mrs. Gertrude Martin
> request the honor of your presence
> at the marriage of Mr. Martin's daughter
>
> Gabrielle Jane ...

When the couple hosts the wedding themselves,
the following may be used:

> The honor of your presence
> is requested at the marriage of
>
> Miss Gabrielle Jane Martin
>
> to
>
> Mr. Jonathan Brown
>
> Saturday, the tenth of June ...

Of course, you are free to word invitations in any
way you wish, and in a fashion that you find most
appropriate. These suggestions function simply as
social guidelines that can help you structure the
wording based on various situations. You may also
wish to talk to the stationer for additional options,
based on situations he/she has encountered over
the years.

Index

T-U-V